For my sons
and my brothers
and also my forefathers

In My Grandfather's House

In My Grandfather's House

Harry N. Abrams, Inc., Publishers, New York

4

In the summer of 1944, more than forty years ago, I visited my Uncle Dirk on the island of Overflakkee. My stay there made a lasting impression on me, and, strangely enough, the older I get the more clearly I can remember those days.

← Here is Uncle Dirk's farmhouse and the two bridges over the Boezem River, which was teeming with sticklebacks. The wide bridge was for the little steam tram that chugged by every two hours. Sometimes if the engineer saw you fishing, he would toss a piece of coal into the water right in front of you.

For people with a bicycle— that is, everyone on the island— the narrow bridge was rather awkward. It didn't matter on which side of the bicycle you walked. It was useless; either you would nearly be pulled off balance* by the usually heavily loaded bicycle, or you would scrape your knuckles along the railing. Nobody dared to cross cycling.

* The islanders always carry a gunny sack with them just in case they happen to come across a meal of onions or potatoes lying about somewhere.

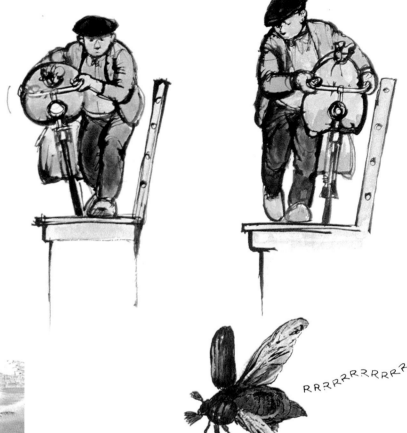

RRRRRRRRRR

If I looked out of my bedroom window (upstairs, on the right) the bridge on the left looked thoroughly cheerful and adventurous and reminded me of a noisy steam whistle! The one on the right was serious, cautious, hesitant. The two bridges always made me think of the biblical picture of the wide and the narrow road.

I also have acute memories of sounds: the buzzing of the colorful beetles flying past us as we walked home after the evening chat on the wharf, and the unpleasant crunching sounds of our footsteps on the gravel when we got home.

Behind that lighted window, where Aunt Marie
was doing her mending, I was given a cup of cocoa,
and then it was off to bed.

7

And once I got upstairs, stood in front of the open window, and looked out into the dark night, I could hear absolutely NOTHING (except for the ticking of my father's watch behind me and very occasionally the splash of a fish in the Boezem). It was wonderful! Hanging over the windowsill, I breathed in the delicious aromas of hay and onions.

Oh, oh, how I loved Flakkee then! (Overflakkee is an island in south Holland and is bounded by the island of Goeree.)

And as the excitement of picturesque country life weren't enough, up in the attic on a bookshelf were three volumes of Dik Trom (the popular adventures of a chubby boy). I can still recall the musty smell of old books mingled with the fragrance of dried apples.

Later, as I drifted into sleep, I thought with a feeling of intense joy of how beautifully everything fit together.

The knowledge that I was spending the night under the same roof as the two cart horses also gave me a contented feeling.

I was a very great admirer of those gentle giants,

↑ those "water drawers"!

(The Dutch word for a strong person or animal is "water drawer." The derivation of this name is rather sad. A kind of finch, also known as "water drawer," used to be kept in a cage and was forced to draw its own drinking water by means of a miniature bucket.)

I am also a great admirer of shire horses,
such as this Zeeland horse and the Belgian horse.

10

I love these horses' bodies.

They lift their hooves with an unexpected grace.

14

Everywhere you could see evidence that there were many horses on the island!
And while boys nowadays have to wait for it to snow before they can pelt each other, on the island there was never any shortage of ammunition.

Flocks of sparrows were attracted to the horse manure and were outlawed because of the damage they did to the corn. Therefore almost every boy had a

No. 2119. **Sparrow trap,** made of fine copper wire with a strong spring. Price 3 ct.

The trap was placed in the horse manure and — bang!
The reward was 2 cents for a sparrow, 1 cent for an egg.

16

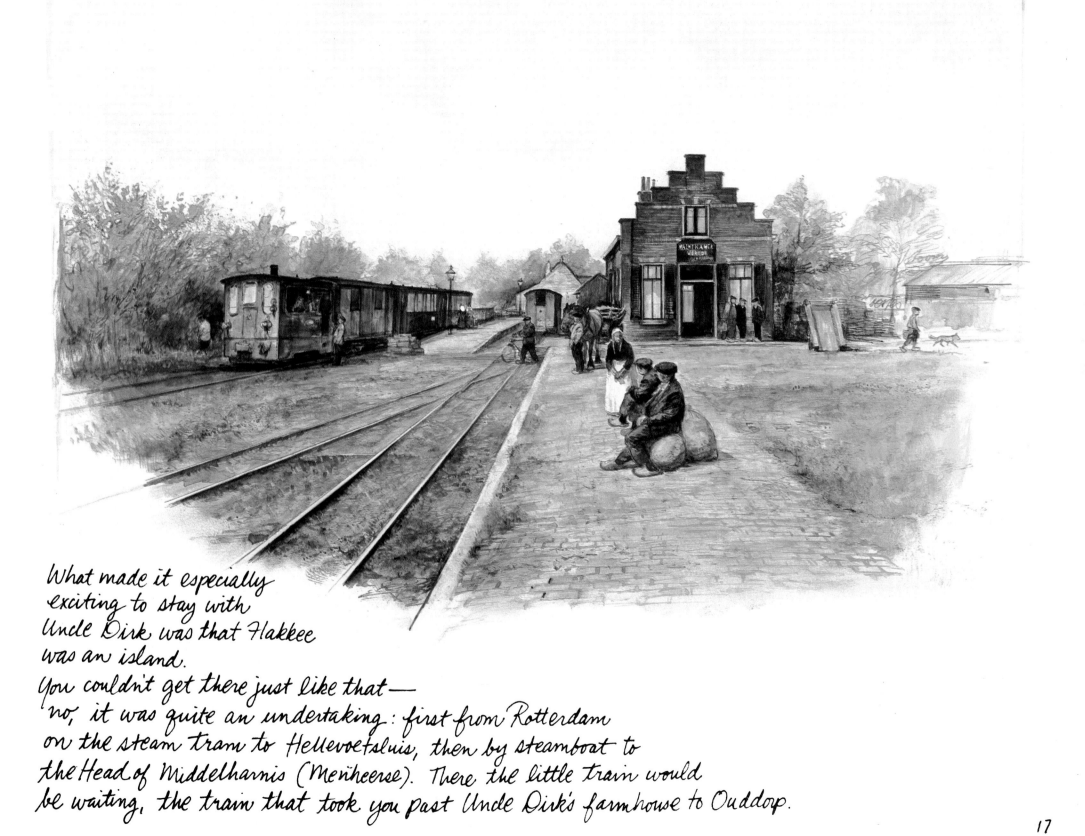

What made it especially
exciting to stay with
Uncle Dirk was that Flakkee
was an island.
You couldn't get there just like that —
no, it was quite an undertaking: first from Rotterdam
on the steam tram to Hellevoetsluis, then by steamboat to
the Head of Middelharnis (Menheerse). There the little train would
be waiting, the train that took you past Uncle Dirk's farmhouse to Ouddorp.

17

the island
Goeree-Overflakkee.

It was inconceivable to think that everything you saw, from great churches to nutmeg graters, had been brought over by boat!

It should have occurred to me when I was staying on the island that my father in his boyhood had spent his holidays with Uncle Dirk, exactly as I was doing.

Perhaps I was too preoccupied with all the new impressions, or perhaps it was just too difficult for a child to look back a generation.

We could be having pleasant talks together about our boyhood vacations, but that is not possible because my father is no longer here.

I could also have had fascinating conversations with my grandfather about Flakkee, but he died when I was five years old.

my grandpa
MARINUS POORTVLIET
1878 - 1938

It must have been around 1900 that my grandfather left the island of Flakkee
to seek his fortune in Rotterdam.
Here he is standing next to his father, old Sakries, in front of the Meyer Hotel in Middelharnis.
Shortly, Marinus will say goodbye to his father and board the steamboat,
and then the die will have been cast.

20

It is also possible that my grandfather did not leave from Menheerse, but that he boarded a barge at Dirksland.

Here you see Marinus walking along the wharf between his father and his mother.
They are coming from Dike Street, where the family lives.

But it's really not important whether my grandfather set sail from Middelharnis or Dirksland. The main point is that around the turn of the century, he left the island of Goeree-Overflakkee, and that was a big step!

The boat is out of sight and Krijna and Sakries are back at home—
they have resumed life as usual.
Meanwhile, the village of Dirksland lies peaceful and unblemished in the snow.

22

The young emigrant
finds the way to his room
through dirty and
noisy streets.

At the end of the day he is at his destination.
And there he is, a country boy in some
back room three flights up.

He will try to learn to speak proper Dutch —
people snickered a bit when he asked
them directions. When he looks
out of the window before
going to bed there is not
a trace of snow.

But as night falls in Dirksland the houses are still
delicately powdered with snow.

Perhaps you are thinking: how do I know it was snowing?
Admittedly, I don't even know the year my grandfather left,
let alone the season.
But I've already painted the picture <u>Farewell on the Wharf</u>
as a snow scene, and now I have to go with it.

Besides, I think that one can take the step of leaving one's
ancestral home much more lightheartedly on a cheerful summer's day

26

Ouddorp

than in winter, when the deserted fields stretch far into the distance
and people seek the comforts of home — a cozy, glowing stove
Brussels sprouts, the oil lamp lit early....

27

28

And what about one of those
← depressing rainy days
when you have to go outside
into the wide world?

Meanwhile the people at home
are comfortably pouring
another cup of coffee.

It's not worth thinking about.

Marinus lies wide awake on the strange bed in the dark just picturing some scenes in his mind.

—

Dike Street in Dirksland, where he grew up—

doing an errand for a neighbor woman who is peering out her door to see what is taking Marien so long—

Perhaps he had to wait for ages in the shop because some villagers in front of him were having a long gossip

31

... about someone in the Voorstraat who was apparently very ill, because straw was being spread out!

(straw would be strewn in front of the house of someone who was seriously ill in order to muffle the sounds of horses and carts going by)

or perhaps he had simply hung around too long watching the blacksmith in the Voorstraat...

where there was always lots of activity

except on the Lord's Day, when everyone went to church.

From near and far,
black figures could
be seen moving in
the direction of
God's house.

36

Some people had to travel
quite a distance.
(In bad weather the
women would not put on
their headdresses until
they were in the village,
where they could stop
at a relative's house.)

One person who was not in the church on Sundays was the young cowherd.

Every day of the week, rain or shine, he would herd his master's cows along the dikes.

He gets up
about half-
past four...

... and then he sets off
with his lunch bag and
water bottle on his way
to the farm.
He will be back home
at six o'clock in the
evening.

he works as hard
as an adult
but often he is
no more than
nine or ten
years old...

Gaiter, a forerunner of the Wellington boot

they were dreadfully long days, during which
the young fellow was
terribly bored
and if by chance anyone
passed by he would
always ask what time
it was...

40

A tough job for such a little fellow.
When the ditches dried up in the summer, the cows would keep
trying to enter the fields with crops — and then just try and
stop them! When it was finally time to go home, he might
have the bad luck of having the wind and the rain blowing
toward him. In that case he couldn't possibly get the cows,
who always turn their backsides to the rain, to go in the right direction.

In Ouddorp the cows from the village were all
allowed to graze together in the dunes.
When the cows came back in the evening, barn
doors and garden gates were hurriedly closed because
the cows had not had an abundance of food in the dunes!

"The cows are coming!" had the same sort of significance
to the villagers as "The Philistines are upon us!"

42

As my cousin Nelly says: the people of Flakkee are noted for being hardworking, and that's because they are taught to work hard from babyhood onward!

43

Children were kept busy—
girls in the usually large
families were accomplished
"deputy mothers."

Sometimes young girls
learned to take complete
charge of the family
after their mother
had died.

They very efficiently brought up a whole string of younger brothers and sisters while father only occasionally came home from the sea.

45

46

It was simply a law:
always keep your hands busy.

Every day, as soon as you
got home from school, the
first thing you did was
knit twenty rows onto
the stocking.
(Everyone wore knitted
stockings.) Mothers who
could afford it sometimes
slipped a copper coin into
the middle of the ball of
wool.
After knitting your
regulation twenty rows
you were allowed to
play outdoors.

47

The Blue House, built in 1659, where Keesje Bok — standing here with his sister — was born.

He well remembers how it was
in his boyhood.
Kees's father had a salmon pen,
a fish trap constructed of beechwood
or osiers, situated on the tidal
mud flats of the Grevelingen.

LAND

300 M

WATER

500 M

HOOK

Twice in every twenty-four hours
the trap had to be inspected, which
meant that as soon as high tide
had receded someone had to
check to see if any salmon had
been left behind in the deeper pool
that was dug inside the hook.

If there weren't many seagulls
circling around (and you could
already see them from the dike),
it was a good sign.

49

In daylight one person could check the trap, but at night it was more difficult. At night father Bok often took Keesje with him on the crossbar of his bicycle. "Whoever can hold a lantern can come along!" Then Keesje had to hold the lantern while his father tried to catch the salmon with a landing net.

Very often Kees stood there half-dozing. Once he even fell asleep and tumbled into the water. The lantern went out and the matches got wet.

In order to catch a salmon with a landing net you had to succeed on your first try because a salmon wouldn't be so easily fooled a second time. If you missed the first time, you had to start the cumbersome business of using a dragnet.

Once the salmon was caught it was hit on the nose with a special piece of wood. A catch of one salmon per tide wasn't bad at all. A winter salmon weighed up to twenty or thirty pounds.

Then it was time to get on the bicycle and go home. Kees on the crossbar in front, the salmon, the boots, some herrings picked up from a different trap were all on the bicycle.

Once they were home Kees could get back into bed and father would pack the salmon in thick straw (there was no ice) in a special basket and bring it quickly to Breen, who brought travelers in his carriage to the Stellendam boat.

Salmon had to be taken to Rotterdam as quickly as possible

The herrings were put into a wheelbarrow and Kees and his sister set off to peddle them door to door.
The price was ten herrings for 10 cents.
It was a tough job finding buyers — some people had just eaten herring, others had just finished cleaning the oil stove, but the real reason was that people had no money.

Sometimes Breen's carriage didn't leave because there were no passengers that day; on those occasions father Bok had to take the salmon to Stellendam himself.

And in those days he was not yet rich enough to buy a bicycle so he had to carry the salmon on foot. It sometimes happened that he wouldn't get back until dawn, when his mother would be waiting for him with his lunch bag. He had to go straight to work on the land.

Throughout the autumn little Kees Bok trudged along the roads looking for chicory roots that had fallen off carts (people made surrogate coffee from the roots).

Even though a farm boy usually walked behind the cart to pick up whatever fell off, you could still sometimes find an odd root.

At home Kees kept the roots that he had found under sand, and at the end of the season he brought them to the factory.

Once, at the end of twenty weeks of searching, Kees was able to earn the princely sum of fl 6.25!

55

My cousin Jan well remembers how as a child he wept as he labored to turn a heavy plow and that there was nobody at all to help him.

When my cousin Nelly left school her father gave her a choice: she could go into service or she could take care of eight cows.

Thus three sisters (17, 15, and 12) were given charge over twenty-four cows.

Their duties were milking, feeding, grinding beets, cleaning out the stalls, churning and selling the milk in the village,

and if the six horses were at work on the land their stables had to be cleaned out too.

keeping busy

While washing
the dishes, you sang.
It was a good way
of learning the
psalm verse for
Monday morning.

And while reading in the
warm room on a winter's evening,
you could get a sizable piece
of knitting done at the same time.

In those days
the saying was
"a horse's mouth and
a woman's hand should
never be still."

There were also many
impoverished and illiterate children who had been
forced to leave school in order to work on the land.

By half past four in the morning the boys were
already walking along the dikes to the farms where
they worked. Often it was an hour's walk.

Their first job of the day was to fetch the horses from
the meadow so that the farmhands
could get straight to work when
they arrived.

Nice cheap workers, those twelve-
year-old lads!

In the evenings on the way home
a boy would often cut himself a
sackful of grass for his rabbits
(he didn't keep them for fun).

59

Sometimes when he got home he would not only be
exhausted but also soaking wet from the rain.
    Then he could sit down in front of the stove
next to his father, who had also just come
    home from work, and the two of them would
    watch the steam rising from their clothes—
        they had no other clothes to put on.

There were also a lot of boys who worked
on the fishing boats, and on Sundays
between church services it was fun
to show your friends which boat
you were working on —

much more fun than the
following morning at
the crack of dawn.

It was hard work at sea,
and it seemed ages before
the week was over and the
ships were back in the harbor.

No. 1770. **Train,** consisting of locomotive with sturdy clockwork mechanism, tender, 2 carriages, and circular rails. 55 cm., rail width 35 mm with brake mechanism. Price £ 1.80

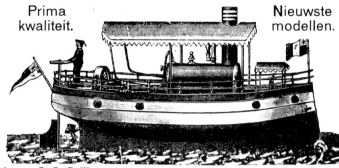

No. 2287. **Steamship,** beautifully executed; the propeller is operated directly by the turbine flywheel in imitation of the original American steam engines. Horizontal copper boiler, regulating tap, movable steering wheel, safety valve, steam whistle, fine deck. The boat is beautifully painted, and the unpainted parts are very smartly nickeled and polished. Length 50 cm. Price £ 6.15

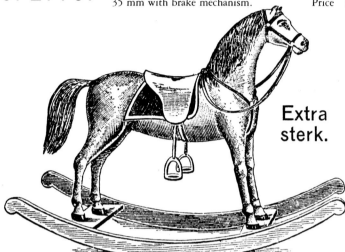

Extra sterk.

No. 2384. **Rocking horse,** extra strong, very sturdily made, with bridle and stirrups. Beautifully painted. Seat height 66 cm, body length 45 cm. Price £ 3.75

Nieuw!

No. 4854. **New! Donkey with rider,** very comical, excellent quality clockwork. Length 19 cm, height 15 cm. Price 72 ct.

Bear, excellent quality clockwork, walks forward, **No. 3323.** painted to look lifelike. Size 14½ x 7 x 4 cm. Price 45 ct.

No. 3360. **Doll,** Movable arms and legs, fixed eyes, colored skirt with jacket, straw hat, wavy hair. Height 24 cm. Price 45 ct.

No. 3353. **Doll,** Doubly movable arms and legs and head that can turn, beautiful sleeping eyes, wavy hair, colored and embellished fabric dress, straw hat, shoes and stockings. Undressable. Height 40½ cm. Price £ 1.90

No. 3363. **Doll,** Movable arms and legs and head that can turn, wavy hair, beautiful black fabric dress edged with lace, sleeping eyes, straw hat, shoes and stockings. Undressable. Height 45½ cm. Price £ 1.75

No. 1776. **Tableware** made of fine porcelain decorated with flowers, consisting of 6 cups, 6 saucers, 2 bread dishes, 1 coffee pot, 1 milk jug, 1 sugar pot, packed in cardboard box. Length 36 cm, width 20½ cm. Price 95 ct.

No. 4850. **Music box,** made of finely decorated tin. Height 11 cm, width 8 cm. Price 15 ct.

64

Even though there were toys, children did not receive very many.

There was usually no money to buy toys, so people made their own.

With the help of a wooden spool children knitted reins;

the bit would be made out of a parcel handle obtained from a clothing warehouse.

After a pig had been slaughtered, the bladder was blown up and dried, and that became a ball.

Put a few pieces of licorice in a bottle, add water, and shake until you have licorice water. These were called master's bottles. In this way you made lemonade.

Rub ears of wheat in your hands, blow away the chaff, and then chew the ears. In this way you got chewing gum.

A great "outing" during school vacation was visiting father in the fields and baking potatoes in their jackets.

Children never tired of a rough-and-tumble chase in the hay.

Another great thrill:
seeing the peddler
walking on his way
as you came out
of school.

The peddler hawked
thread, ribbon,
and bits and bobs
that he carried in
a large box with
a shoulder strap.

67

Old Johnnie sometimes came with his
handcart from Menheerse calling,

"Shrimps, shrimps, one cent a bowlful!"

One man even came
all the way from Brabant
with a dogcart full of
pots and pans.

My grandfather certainly remembers the Jewish merchant with his cart full of nuts... and how some unkind boys tipped over the cart by dropping an enormous red cabbage onto it.

The furious merchant rushed into the barn and up to the loft, but the boys had already made their escape down a rope.

Thinking about his Flakkee, my grandfather must have felt homesick when visions such as these crossed his mind.

The lamplighter was also the town crier. If there was a strong wind he held his opened coat around the lantern while lighting the lamp.

No one was ever surprised to see a large pig loose on the street followed by someone on a bicycle. It was a common sight — the boar had simply been ordered somewhere.

In front of the inn a gentleman — a traveling salesman or an itinerant tailor is waiting for his hired porter.

Another everyday sight: the old men on the wharf,
talking nineteen to the dozen, watching everything
that goes on.
As a child you always had to be careful when you
    passed them by, or before you knew it
    you had a splotch of tobacco juice on your leg.

The undertaker's messenger in his top hat with a long black crepe veil that hung down over one arm.

a town policeman

a state policeman

"On behalf of the family you are notified of the death of Jan Pieter," etc., etc.
Once the muttered speech was over, you said, "Thank you for the message, my compliments."

the rubbish cart

the gas cart

a common sight in those days — people with backs stooped from hard work

The handsome farm carts
that you saw in use everywhere
were usually drawn by two horses.

Sometimes they were drawn
by only one horse if there
wasn't much of a load...
like on the first of March. It was the custom that farm laborers
who lived in the farmhand's cottage next to the farm changed
employers on March first.

There was a great upheaval in the island population on that day, as though everyone were on the move.

The whole kit and caboodle was piled on the cart in one go.

In the new home there would already be fresh straw spread out on the beds (the beds were built into the houses) so that it was only a matter of putting on the bedclothes, and that was that.

All the crops were brought in from the fields by horse and cart. In order to load up an extra large amount of hay or corn people would make use of a railing to which a wooden boom could be attached as a lever.

Sweet little harvest mice would always come out from under the hay.

When it was time to harvest the sugar beets, the sides of the cart would be raised by specially fitted "beet holders."

What a mess there was at sugar beet harvest time! The carts drove back and forth loaded with sugar beets, and the village was covered in mush!

On the winter street the pulp stretched from pavement to pavement, and sometimes you <u>had</u> to go out to shop

When sugar beet harvest was over everybody had a good scrub on the Friday before Christmas!

79

People drew water from the church canal or from the pump— there were no waterworks in those days.

Fetching water was quite an undertaking. Sometimes in the summer it was even necessary for a water boat to come. The town crier would announce its arrival.

People didn't waste water— first the spinach was washed in it until the sand had sunk down to the bottom, and then it became bath water. Everyone went into the tub— the smallest first.

There was no sewage system either.

What practically everyone _did_ have was a pig!

You simply couldn't manage without a pig; it was your savings account — the family capital and the ticket to survive the coming winter.

Every spring a new piglet was acquired.

81

Every house had a pigsty.

↓ In the beginning it was far too big for the piglet,

but at the end of the pig's short and boring life there was not much room left over. By then the pig weighed about five hundred pounds!

Visitors always had to come and look at the pig!

Following the plow and picking up seed potatoes for the pig!

Some flour with boiled seed potatoes.

The pig was
well looked
after.

following the
reapers and
gleaning ears
of wheat

83

But in November it was all over for him!

After the butcher had slaughtered the pig, it was covered in straw that was set on fire in order to burn off the hairs.

This instrument was used for scraping the pig; the hook was for pulling off the hooves. The children stood around waiting for these delicacies plus the half-charred tail.

Once again there was bacon hanging from the rafters!

Sometimes the pig was slaughtered in haste —
for example, when there was swine fever going around,
and the pig didn't look well.
The meat was not officially tested — the easiest thing
to do was to give some meat to the village simpleton, and
then keep an eye on him for a few days.

This was the working man's cow—another valuable possession!
With goat's milk, home-cured bacon, and some home-grown vegetables a person was practically self-sufficient.

There was no trace of that familiar country way of life in the Rotterdam of 1900.

My grandfather must have missed the local costume too.

The women of Flakkee wore this crocheted cap as everyday wear.

On Sundays you got dressed up: then you wore the lace headdress with gold spirals and pins.

It is often said that local costume is not affordable nowadays, but a costume and jewelry that lasted a lifetime were a lot cheaper than the folly of following the latest fashion. ↱

89

The
women
wore shawls
instead
of
coats.

The men wore a suit like this.

When working in the fields they wore old clothes, brown fustian trousers and a shirt.

This man is brewing coffee in the fields — some dry straw in a ditch and a match.

— The shirts were mended a hundred times.

After making coffee, some people would put a snare in the ashes: hares liked to sit in the ashes at night!

If the men got overheated they took off their trousers, and after work they walked home still dressed in their long underwear.

92

My grandfather used to work
on the land doing all these things
before he went to Rotterdam.

"One, two, heave-ho!"
and then you had a
150-pound sack on your neck.

It wasn't that my grandfather left the country to get away from hard work —

in Rotterdam he began work as a plasterer,

one of the toughest trades!

Cousin Jaap inherited the trade through his father from grandfather.

My grandfather couldn't forget Goeree-Overflakkee
In the evenings he would paint these pictures.

Of course he didn't forget his parents either,
and from time to time he would write them a letter.

my great-grandparents
Sacharias Poortvliet and
Krijna Poortvliet de Bonte
in the year 1900.

The previous year, 1899, their daughter Cornelia had died at the age of 33, and since then my great-grandmother always looked so sad.

On the wall hangs the commemorative painting that their son Leendert Willem (grandfather's brother) made for his parents to mark their fortieth wedding anniversary.

29.FEBR:1856.

1896 FEBR:29.

S. POORTVLIET.

K. DE BONTE.

Ter gedachtenis aan het veertigjarig huwelijksfeest mijner GELIEFDE OUDERS, uw dankbaren zoon

L.W. POORTVLIET.

The romance that blossomed between Krijna de Bonte and the adventurer Sacharias began with the potato blight of 1846.

Like many others, Krijna's father was forced by poverty to sell his farm; thus Krijna went from farmer's daughter to a lower level on the social scale.

No. 4

In het jaar een duizend acht honderd zes en vijftig, den *negen en twintig* der maand *Februarij* zijn voor ons ondergeteekende *Pieter Laajer, Burgemeester* Ambtenaar van den burgerlijken-stand der gemeente D I R K S L A N D, Provincie Zuidholland, in het huis der gemeente, in het openbaar en in tegenwoordigheid der natenoemene getuigen, verschenen *Sacharias Poortvliet* oud *drie en dertig* jaren, van beroep *avonturier* geboren te *Dirksland* en wonende te *Dirksland* ~~meer~~ derjarige zoon van *Cornelis Poortvliet en van Elizabeth Groen, beiden overleden*

En *Krijna de Bonte* oud *negentien* jaren, van beroep *Zonder* geboren te *Dirksland* en wonende te ~~Dirksland~~ ~~min~~ derjarige dochter van *Krijn de Bonte en van Cornelia Breeknee, beiden overleden,*

welke ons verzocht hebben tot de voltrekking van hun voorgenomen huwelijk te willen overgaan daartoe aan ons ter hand stellende *hunne geboorte-acten, de overlijdens-acten van de ouders, de grootouders van vaderszijde en den grootvader van moederszijde der bruid, het bewijs dat de Bruidegom aan zijne verpligtingen ten opzigte der Nationale Militie heeft voldaan, eene notariële acte, waarbij Geertrui Overdijk als grootmoeder van moederszijde hare volkomen toestemming tot dit huwelijk geeft en den certificaat waaruit blijkt dat de beide huwelijksafkondigingen in de gemeente Herkingen op den zeventienden en den vier en twintigsten dezer maand zonder stuiting hebben plaats gehad, terwijl dezelve op die dagen ook in deze gemeente ongehinderd zijn afgeloopen.*

Dien ten gevolge en nadat de bruidegom en bruid elk afzonderlijk aan ons ambtenaar van den Burgerlijken-stand, op onze daartoe gedane afvraging hadden verklaard, dat zij elkander aannemen tot echtgenoten, en dat zij getrouwelijk alle de pligten zullen vervullen, welke door de wet aan den huwelijken staat verbonden zijn, hebben wij in naam der wet verklaard, dat de personen van

Sacharias Poortvliet en Krijna de Bonte

bovengemeld, door den echt aan elkander zijn verbonden.

Van al hetwelk wij deze akte hebben opgemaakt in tegenwoordigheid van *Leendert Kardux oud een en veertig jaren bouwman, behuwdbroeder van de bruid Jacol Heijboer oud zeven en dertig jaren, bouwknecht, behuwd broeder van den bruidegom, Cornelis Koert oud zes en veertig jaren bouwman en Arij van der Ent oud drie en dertig jaren, bode, bekenden van de comparanten, allen wonende te Dirksland, die na voorlezing met ons ende comparanten hebben geteekend.*

← Marriage certificate of Sacharias and Krijna de Bonte. She was nineteen and he was thirty-three. They married in Dirksland in 1856.

It often happened that rich farmers' daughters sat working year in and year out on their trousseaus — but remained unmarried.

101

Birth certificate of Sacharias, →
born on February 8, 1823, at 11:00 p.m.,
in Dirksland. His father, Cornelis,
was thirty-five.

"my great-grandfather" →

SACHARIAS POORTVLIET

geboren te Dirksland 8-2-1823
overleden . " 26-12-1903

Sach: Poortvliet

Death certificate of Sacharias Poortvliet. →
He died on December 26, 1903,
at the age of eighty.

In het jaar een duizend acht honderd drie en twintig, den *Tienden* der maand *Februarij* des *voor*middags ten *Negen* uren, is voor ons Schout en gecommitteerd Ambtenaar tot het werk van den Burgerlijken Staat der Gemeente *Dirksland*, verschenen *Cornelis Voortvliet* oud *Vijf en dertig* jaren, van beroep *Arbeider* wonende *alhier* welke ons heeft verklaard, dat *Zijne huisvrouw Elizabeth Groen* op den *Agsten dezer* des *avonds* ten *Elf* uren, bevallen is van een kind van het *man* lijk geslacht, hetwelk hij zegt de voorna*am* te zullen dragen van *Sacharias*

De gemelde verklaring is geschiedt in tegenwoordigheid van *Arend de Bruin Veertig* oud *jaren*, van beroep *Arbeider* wonende *Alhier* en van *Joost Stuberge* oud *even en twintig* jaren, van beroep *Veldwagter* wonende *alhier*.

En hebben de comparanten deze Akte, na voorlezing, met ons geteekend.

De Schout en gecommitteerd Ambtenaar voornoemd,

He was the fifth Sacharias born out of the marriage of Cornelis and Elizabeth — the previous four little Sachariases died in the cradle before they were one year old.

Nº 50   Akte van OVERLIJDEN van

Sacharias Voortvliet.

In het jaar een duizend negen honderd drie, den *zeven twintigsten* der maand *December* zijn voor ons ondergeteekende, Ambtenaar van den Burgerlijken-Stand der gemeente **Dirksland**, verschenen: *Leunis van der Huijs* oud *rijf en zestig* jaren, van beroep *gemeente bode* en *Hendrik Mathijs Boordzand* oud *zes en dertig* jaren, van beroep *timmerman* wonende beiden in deze gemeente, die ons hebben verklaard, dat op den *zeven twintigsten* der maand *December* duizend negen honderd drie, des *voormiddags* te *drie* uren, in het huis staande in deze gemeente, numero *drie honderd drie en twintig* **is overleden** *Sacharias Voortvliet* van beroep *landbouwer* geboren te *Dirksland* en wonende te *Dirksland* in den ouderdom van *tachtig jaren* geboren in het jaar *achttien honderd drie en tachtig, zoon van Cornelis Voortvliet en van Elizabeth Groen, beiden overleden, echtgenoot van Hijna de Bonte, zonder beroep, wonende te Dirksland*

En hebben wij hiervan deze akte opgemaakt, die na voorlezing is onderteekend door ons en de declaranten.

1823

In those days a midwife charged fl. 2.50 for delivering a baby.

A doctor's house call in the village cost thirty cents; a visit out in the polder cost one guilder.

Six years before, the velocipede had been invented, but it was of no use on the bad roads around Dirksland.

In Sakries's family six babies had already died.

Little Sakries survived, but he always stayed small. Throughout his life he never weighed more than one hundred pounds, and he wore children's clogs.

In 1828 Dirksland had 1,494 inhabitants.

ℤ, z, z, Z, z, Z.

ZACHARIAS AT THE SEA

How amazing, so much water!
At the very sight I quake—
Yet brave folks sail away upon it
As if it were a little lake!

Although in this schoolbook Zacharias is shown dressed like this, my great-grandfather and his friends wore shabby clothes. There was much poverty in Dirksland at that time. Even a new skirt wasn't affordable, so every year the women took a strip of new fabric as wide as the back opening of their apron and turned the skirt to show the new fabric.

What are the boys talking about in 1839? About the recent invention of the camera obscura? I think not. They are most probably talking about the impending opening of the first Dutch iron railway on September 20!

There was a friend of the family who had a wooden leg, and after the right shoe on his foot wore out he would wear the left one.

Dried cow manure was used as fuel.

And the lamp was often hung tilted to catch the last drops of oil.

They
are ever
quiet
and
contented.

It is interesting to compare the beginning and the end of the general report for 1850.

GENERAL REPORT FOR THE COUNTY COUNCIL
OF DIRKSLAND IN THE YEAR 1850

I. COUNCIL ADMINISTRATION

a. What are the principal occupations of the Inhabitants?

Farming

b. Have these occupations in general had a favorable outcome or were there setbacks?

The results have been extremely unfavorable through the failure of crops.

c. Are the Inhabitants quiet and contented; if not, what particular grievances are there, and what can be done to allay these grievances?

They are ever quiet and contented.

II. PARTICULARS
Items not covered under the previous headings and General Remarks.

There is always much poverty.

Aldus opgemaakt te Dirksland den 22 January 1850

Burgemeester en Assessoren,

(get.) P. Laayer

Forsedommente van derelog

(get.) Jacob de Graaff L.S.

e. What is the condition of the roads and the bridges connected with them?

The roads are generally made of heavy clay and thus are bad in the winter; the bridges are in good condition.

f. Are the roads that communicate with neighboring Municipalities always in a usable condition?

During the winter they are practically unusable.

Sacharias did
a great deal of
walking.

My great-grandfather's profession was adventurer.
He used to buy up the "tenths" in advance (the "tenths" were one tenth of a total crop,
with which rent or tax was paid). As well as that he had a sack-rental business,
did some crop farming, and had a few farm animals.

Because he also did a bit of dealing in livestock, he tramped over half the island looking for bargains. Here he is going somewhere accompanied by two sons— Cornelis (with beard), who was a butcher, and Dirk.

The journey was often to Ouddorp, where fishermen's wives,
in order to earn extra money, would fatten up a second pig for sale —
aside from the pig they kept for their own consumption.

That was a walk of
twenty-five miles there and back
in one day.

While you were walking you heard only your own footsteps.
And at night it was pitch black.

Thus when people made an appointment for an evening visit, they took into account the phase of the moon.

The trip from here to school is a good long way.

" Mother, my new clogs still hurt !"
And then you were hustled outside with
the cheerful advice : "Play a lot."

One never really thinks about it,
but how long did a farm laborer's pair of clogs last ?
Four to five weeks ! Then they were worn out.

All that walking
was greatly reduced
once the bicycle arrived.

115

Not only do they get you to your destination in the twinkling of an eye
but also on the way you have
a great opportunity to look
into other people's houses!

And people love
to do that!

Meanwhile from behind the lace curtains, people are looking out to see what those two outside are up to.

My great-grandparents lived on Dike Street (Straatdiek Dirksland 197)

Krijna and Sacharias's house

Sannetje's Wittekoek's candy shop, where you could buy "a pennyworth" from the counter

Brammetje Dunweg's shop. He sold oil lamps.

Smith's alley

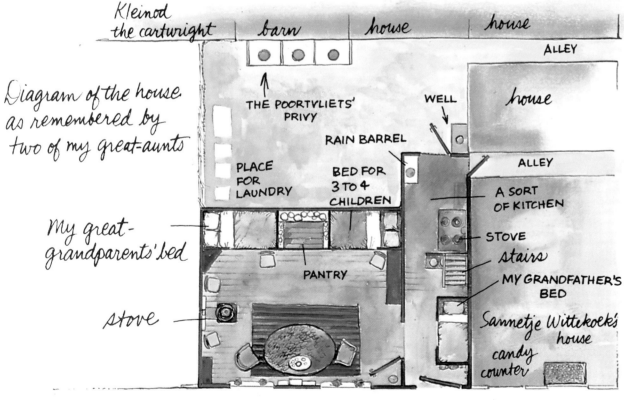

Kleinod the cartwright

barn

house

house

ALLEY

Diagram of the house as remembered by two of my great-aunts

THE POORTVLIETS' PRIVY

WELL

house

RAIN BARREL

PLACE FOR LAUNDRY

BED FOR 3 TO 4 CHILDREN

ALLEY

A SORT OF KITCHEN

My great-grandparents' bed

PANTRY

STOVE

stairs

MY GRANDFATHER'S BED

stove

Sannetje Wittekoek's house

candy counter

When it was evening and the notorious privy bucket (or old preserving jar) was full it was simply emptied into the Spuie.

a great-aunt: "Granny, what shall I do now?"
"Go and cut up paper for the little house."

In the spinde (a pantry a little below floor level) the so-called stoneware was kept. A few steps down were the little cellars beneath the built-in beds.

The gin bottle was also kept in the pantry. Sakries always had a shot before going to sleep. He drank it standing in the pantry.

Dutch gin

Here the winter supplies were kept. There was a musty smell in the beds that emanated from the potatoes in the cellar below.

After the death of her mother at thirty-three great-aunt Lenie often stayed with her grandpa and grandma.

Peeking out between the curtains of her bed Lenie had a good view of everything: Sakries took off his clothes and socks, leaving his underwear on; took the chamber pot from the bed shelf, placed it on the ground, and climbed into bed.

My great-grandmother would take off the headdress (which she wore every day) and drape it over a vase. Then she took off her black dress and stockings and put on a nightgown.

She blew out the oil lamp and lit the night light on the mantelpiece.

People used to go to bed at about 9:00 p.m. and get up at 4:30 a.m.

The cabinet was my great-grandmother's pride and joy. In it she kept her headdresses, gold jewelry, linens, and valuable documents.

the children's bed

In those days children often slept three or four to a bed. At night you might suddenly hear: "One, two, three — together!" and then everyone would turn over simultaneously.

My grandfather's bed was in the corridor, and he used to like to hang on the doorway and swing himself into bed. But once when he came home late he forgot that a great-aunt was staying and sleeping in his bed.

121

One of the first morning chores was making coffee.

In order to do this my great-grandmother fetched water from the rain barrel.

For scrubbing and washing you used water from the well— that was ground water.

One bucket contained rainwater for drinking, the other contained well water for washing your hands.

the stairs leading to the attic where the boys slept

Once she had the coffee warming on the oil burner, she went to empty the chamber pots.

Then she would pin a cloth to her chest and prepare the bread. First the butter was spread on, then a slice was cut, and so on.

Psalm LXVIII

Psalm 68

Have faith in the Lord with greatest awe!
He bestows his favors on us day by day:
The Lord is our salvation. Who would
not praise the highest Majesty with the
greatest awe? The Lord is the Lord of our
salvation; He gives us endless goodness.

He gives us eternal life in paradise; He can
and shall give us the perfect solution in
time of need even unto the coming of death.

On Sunday evenings my great-grandfather would take off his cap and say, "Now we'll have some singing."

My great-grandparents were churchgoers as was usual in those days. Sacharias was even a "Notable," as can be seen from the old church registers.

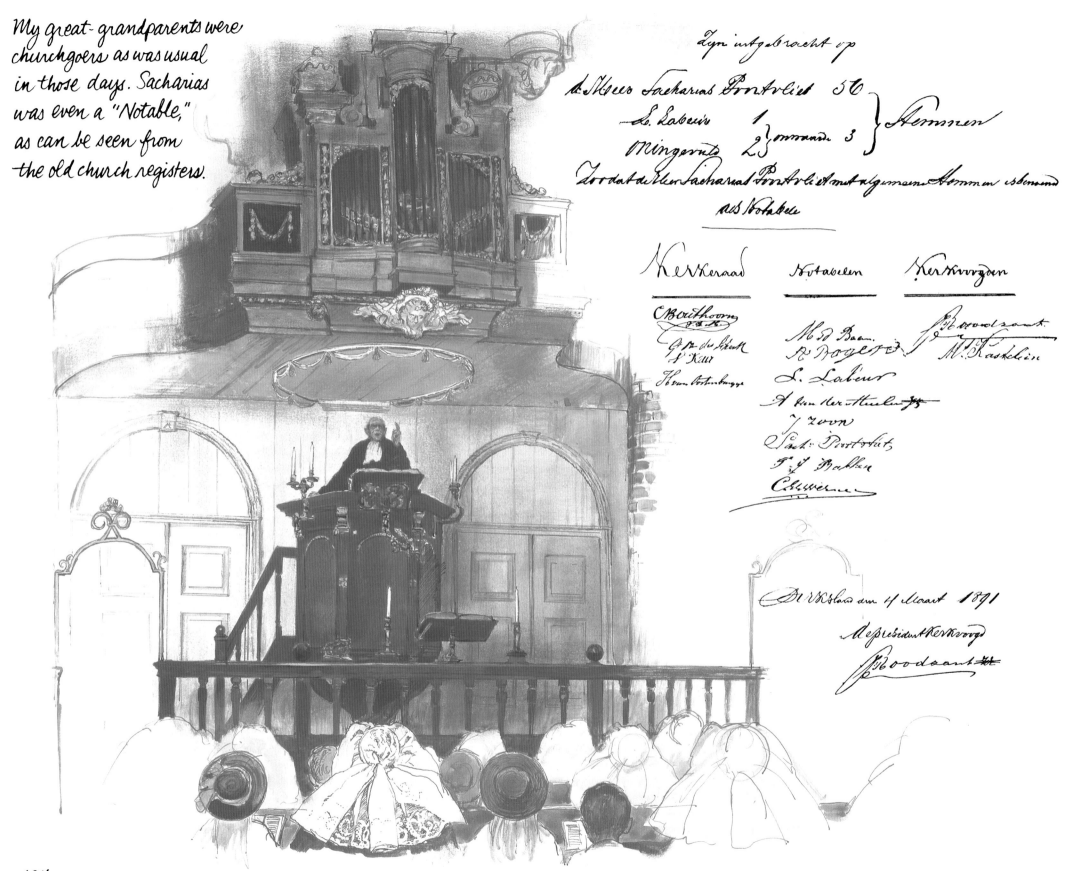

When he was sitting in the →
church on Sundays, my grandfather
had a view of this christening font, which
was at the bottom of the pulpit.

My grandfather Marinus and his father,
Sacharias, were christened from this font.

Den 2ᵈᵉⁿ Maart 1823.

Doopnaam.   Geboortedag ~ Ouders ~ Getuigen.

Sacharias. . . . Geb. den 8 February

V. Cornelis Poortvliet
M. Elizabeth Groen   ← christening record of Sacharias Poortvliet
G. De Ouders.   (born 2/8/1823, christened 3/2/1823)

125

My great-grandfather died on Boxing Day 1903; my great-grandmother survived him by eleven years. During that time she often visited her son Dirk.

In order to spend as much time as possible on Flakkee, my grandfather would take on lengthy plastering jobs on the island. He and a couple of his sons would then stay with his brother Dirk.

Uncle Dirk's farm ↓

When I myself was allowed to stay there (about fifty years later), hardly anything had changed. Perhaps the Vroonweg (the road past the farm) had received a hard surface in the meantime.

128

Thank goodness that the scenic tranquillity of old Flakkee remains unchanged.
I love to look at such places as this.

I also enjoy watching the inhabitants of Flakkee. They are always busy doing something or other. What I love most of all is that delicious Flakkee dialect!

130

When I see the Ruisdael-like landscapes I think that my grandfather should never have left the island.

Just when I was trying to envision how things looked in grandpa's youth, with the help of the memories of my great-aunts (Aunt Dikje) and some old brown snapshots, a wonderful gift dropped in my lap: the family tree!

Armed with the information obtained from old church registers, council archives, and Public Record Office archives, I shall proceed in the search for my forefathers.

I will do it this way: I shall call my actual grandfather, grandfather (1); his father will be grandfather (2), and so on. (I can't be bothered with all that business of "great-great-great.")

SIMON JANSZE POORTVLIET

Chr. Colijnsplaat 1/16/1684;
dec. Dirksland 10/31/1730; mar. (1) c. 1704
Pieternella Pieterdr. van der Berge

1. Jan—chr. Colijnsplaat 5/31/1705
2. Pieter—chr. Colijnsplaat 8/22/1706
3. Jannes—chr. Colijnsplaat 10/16/1707
4. **CORNELIS**—born c. 1709
5. Pieternella—chr. Dirksland 9/10/1716
6. Lena—chr. Dirksland 9/10/1719
7. Lena—chr. Dirksland 12/22/1722
8. Simon—chr. Dirksland 12/9/1724
9. stillborn child, buried Dirksland 4/26/1726
10. Hendrina—chr. Dirksland 7/30/1729
11. Simon—chr. Dirksland 2/6/1731

mijn opa³⁾ **CORNELIS ADRIAENSZ POORTVLIET**

Confirmation Colijnsplaat 4/10/1610;
dec. c. 8/18/1649;
mar. to (1) presumably one Cornelia

1. **JAN CORNELIS**
2. Adriaen
3. Neelken Cornelis
4. Stijnken Cornelis
5. presumably Marijnis
mar. (2) Magdalena van Gelder

mijn opa⁸⁾ **JAN CORNELIS (VAN) POORTVLIET**

Dec. Colijnsplaat 12/7/1650;
mar. c. 1629 Cornelia (Neelken) Adriaans;
church member Colijnsplaat, 1634

1. Adriaan—chr. Colijnsplaat 10/13/1630
2. Cornelis—chr. Colijnsplaat 4/25/1632
3. Cornelis—chr. Colijnsplaat 8/2/1634
4. Cornelis—chr. Colijnsplaat 10/12/1636
5. Lijsbeth Jans—no record of christening found
6. Dirck—chr. Colijnsplaat 1/27/1639
7. Jasper—chr. Colijnsplaat 7/14/1641
8. Jacob—chr. Colijnsplaat 7/14/1641
9. Cornelia—chr. Colijnsplaat 9/15/1647
10. **JAN**—chr. Colijnsplaat 6/19/1650

opa⁵⁾ **CORNELIS SYMONSZ POORTVLIET**

Born c. 1709; dec. Dirksland 3/23/1772;
mar. (1) Dirksland 2/24/1736, 3/18/1736 Maatje
Zachariasdr. van der Groeff, dec. Dirksland 11/24/1749

1. Pieternel—chr. Dirksland 1/20/1737; dec.
   Dirksland 9/15/1741
2. **ZACHARIAS**—chr. Dirksland 10/19/1738
3. Neeltje—chr. Dirksland 10/29/1740; dec.
   Dirksland 11/10/1772
4. Pieternel—chr. Dirksland 10/5/1743
5. Arent—chr. Dirksland 9/4/1745; mar. (2)
   Dirksland 1/5/1750, 2/22/1750 Burgje Johannis van Laa,
   chr. Dirksland 10/19/1705, dec. Dirksland 1/17/1758
6. Cornelia—chr. Dirksland 9/12/1751; dec.
   Dirksland 10/27/1756
7. Johannes—chr. Dirksland 10/14/1753
8. Cornelia—chr. Dirksland 1/4/1756; dec.
   Dirksland 6/11/1757
9. death of a child (?)
10. Lena—chr. Dirksland 6/10/1759; dec.
    Dirksland 2/16/1764
11. Clijntje—chr. Dirksland 3/29/1761;
    dec. Dirksland 6/14/1764
12. Cornelia—chr. Dirksland 3/27/1763
13. Lena—chr. Dirksland 4/14/1765
14. Lena—chr. Dirksland 11/30/1766

opa⁷⁾ **JAN JANSZ POORTVLIET**

Chr. Colijnsplaat 6/19/1650;
church member Colijnsplaat 1672; address Oostagterstraat;
dec. after 6/4/1724; mar. c. 1670 Pieternella Simons
Belleman, chr. Colijnsplaat 10/13/1647

1. Jan—chr. Colijnsplaat 6/28/1671
2. Simon—chr. Colijnsplaat 12/4/1672
3. Marij—chr. Colijnsplaat 4/15/1675
4. Cornelis—chr. Colijnsplaat 6/20/1677
5. Pieter—chr. Colijnsplaat 4/28/1680
6. Adriaan—chr. Colijnsplaat 10/26/1681
7. **SIMON**—chr. Colijnsplaat 1/16/1684
8. Cornelis—chr. Colijnsplaat 3/31/1686
9. Pieter—chr. Colijnsplaat 2/13/1689
10. Jacob—chr. Colijnsplaat 3/18/1691

opa 4) **ZACHARIAS POORTVLIET**

Chr. Dirksland 10/19/1738; dec. Dirksland 11/28/1807; mar. Dirksland 1/20/1769, 2/19/1769 Geertje Cornelis Kluyt, b. Dirksland 11/5/1747, dec. Dirksland 6/2/1810

1. Maatje—chr. Dirksland 12/30/1770; dec. Dirksland 7/14/1773
2. Antje—chr. Dirksland 5/10/1772; dec. Dirksland 2/15/1773
3. Frederik—chr. Dirksland 2/19/1775; dec. Dirksland 2/10/1777
4. Cornelis—chr. Dirksland 3/3/1776
5. Frederik—chr. Dirksland 10/26/1777; dec. Dirksland 1/8/1785
6. Cornelis—chr. Dirksland 10/25/1778; dec. Dirksland 4/11/1783
7. Cornelis—chr. Dirksland 7/27/1783
8. Cornelia—chr. Dirksland 7/27/1783; dec. Dirksland 8/4/1783
9. Frederik—chr. Dirksland 5/8/1785; dec. Dirksland 3/13/1801
10. **CORNELIS**—chr. Dirksland 4/22/1787

opa 3) **CORNELIS POORTVLIET**

B. Dirksland 4/22/1787; dec. Dirksland 1/31/1855; mar. Dirksland 4/13/1809 Elisabeth de Groene, chr. Oud Beijerland 6/6/1786, dec. Dirksland 9/30/1851

1. Zacharias—b. Dirksland 12/10/1809; dec. Dirksland 8/2/1810
2. Zacharias—b. Dirksland 4/14/1811; dec. Dirksland 6/30/1811
3. Sacharias—b. Dirksland 8/27/1812, dec. Dirksland 8/27/1812
4. Geertje—b. Dirksland 9/16/1813; dec. Dirksland 9/16/1813
5. Frederik—b. Dirksland 7/22/1814; dec. Dirksland 7/23/1814
6. Maatje—b. Dirksland c. 1815; dec. Melissant 9/13/1834
7. Sacharias—b. Dirksland 2/19/1817; dec. Dirksland 7/12/1817
8. Jannetje—b. Dirksland 11/14/1818
9. Geertje—b. Dirksland 2/13/1820
10. **SACHARIAS**—b. Dirksland 2/8/1823
11. Gerrit—b. Dirksland 10/23/1825; dec. Dirksland 2/5/1855

opa 2) **SACHARIAS POORTVLIET**

B. Dirksland 2/8/1823; dec. Dirksland 12/26/1903; mar. Dirksland 2/29/1856; dec. Dirksland 8/1914

1. Elisabeth—b. Dirksland 1/3/1857
2. Krijn—b. Dirksland 9/16/1858; dec. Dirksland 10/5/1859
3. Cornelis—b. Dirksland 7/14/1860
4. Krijn—b. Dirksland 12/3/1862
5. Jannetje—b. Dirksland 2/21/1865
6. Cornelia—b. Dirksland 10/1/1867
7. Maarten—b. Dirksland 7/20/1870
8. Gerrit—b. Dirksland 2/1/1873
9. Leendert Willem—b. Dirksland 9/4/1875
10. **MARINUS**—b. Dirksland 4/1/1878
11. Dirk—b. Dirksland 8/24/1880

mijn opa **MARINUS POORTVLIET**

B. Dirksland 4/1/1878; dec. 7/28/1938; mar. Rotterdam 10/2/1901 Rookje Spierdijk Ritmeester, b. 8/6/1877

1. Jacob Spierdijk—b. Rotterdam 2/6/1904
2. **ZACHARIAS**—b. Rotterdam 3/26/1905
3. Cornelis—b. Rotterdam 1/9/1910
4. Jacoba—b. Rotterdam 7/14/1911
5. Leendert Willem—b. Rotterdam 6/7/1913
6. Marinus—b. Rotterdam 7/2/1917
7. Catharina—b. Rotterdam

mijn vader **ZACHARIAS POORTVLIET**

B. Rotterdam 3/26/1905; dec. 3/4/1973; mar. Rotterdam 7/2/1930 Cornelia Hermina de Boer, b. 6/19/1911

1. **MARINUS** Harm—b. Schiedam 8/7/1932
2. Harm—b. Schiedam 8/29/1935; dec. 3/14/1936
3. Harm—b. Schiedam 2/13/1937
4. Karel—b. Schiedam 5/29/1945
5. Hans—b. Schiedam 6/13/1947

MARINUS HARM POORTVLIET

B. Schiedam 8/7/1932; mar. Rotterdam Cornelia Bouman, b. Pernis 2/15/1933

1. Harm—b. Schiedam 3/10/1957; mar. Baarn 9/8/78 Wiepkjen Wagenaar, b. 9/13/1957
    1. Annemarijn—b. Soest 9/1/1986
2. Ronald—b. Schiedam 11/7/1958; mar. Soest 12/23/1983, Irene Louise Slingerland, b. 11/4/1960
    1. Suzanne Louise—b. Soest 5/30/1983
    2. Charlie-Robinson—b. 5/21/1986

When my grandparents (4) Zacharias and Geertje had their son **CORNELIS** christened they had already lost eight children.

A few weeks later there was a sensational arrest at the Goejanverwelle jail, but they really weren't interested. The most important thing was that this Cornelis (their fourth) survived.

april 22 1787

This is the sort of bonnet worn by women at that time. Later it evolved into the local costume headdress.

1850

1875

1900

The somber black dress came later.

In the daytime Cornelis lay in his cradle (wretched things— much too close to the ground— always a draft!).

the "flokkers" (pacifiers)

At night the little one slept in a stuffy built-in bed above the unwashed feet of his parents.

When he cried his mother gave him a "flokker." To make a flokker, you soaked bread in milk, then added sugar. This mixture was piled on top of square pieces of cotton, which were then tied shut with a thread.

If the child continued to cry, the "flokker" would be dipped in brandy. And when the baby was about four months old, poppy seed would be added to the flokker mixture. (In other words, the baby was simply drugged.)

Wet diapers were not washed, just dried and reused.

135

On February 27th, 1795, his eyes nearly fell out of his head in astonishment! (Just like mine in 1940.)

French occupational troops, 221 men strong, arrived in Dirksland to be billeted there, but for some reason they moved on to Goedereede.

At that time Dirksland had 1,151 inhabitants.

In the first years of his life Cornelis was dressed as a girl, as was the custom in those days.

This damned business was of course discussed at great length by the old men. →

They had plenty to talk about: the abolition of the rack (an instrument of torture) in 1798, the great fire in Sommelsdijk in 1799, the fine new organ acquired by the Dirksland church in 1804,

↓

Napoleon's official entry into The Hague in June 1806

In those days you had to pay a tax even for keeping a dog.

For each hunting dog, __three guilders__.
For every other dog, wharf dog, or house dog, __thirty five-cent pieces__

Done in The Hage, under the great seal attached on the ninth day of October, in the year of our Lords and Saviors, one thousand eight hundred and four.

G. B. Emants

Of the ten children, Cornelis is the only one left when, in November 1807, he walked next to his mother behind the bier carrying his father's coffin.

Cornelis was twenty years old.

He didn't sit at home with his mother every evening. He got to know Elizabeth de Groene, and they got on so well, in fact, that they had to marry in haste.

notice of marriage

138

Christening day

The 10th of the Wintermonth....Zacharias....Born November 28

F. Cornelis Poortvliet

M. Elisabeth Groen

Their first child only reached the age of eight months.

Zacharias...... born 7 April 1811

Christening witness:

Pieternella van Opstal

This child died at the age of two and a half months.

The third and the fourth little Sachariases also died in the cradle. Those people wept many tears together.

DEPARTEMENT DES BOUCHES DE LA MEUSE.

ARRONDISSEMENT DE Brielle

COMMUNE De Dirksland.

And the young day laborer could do plenty of brooding in the deathly silence of the wide polders.

Here you see Cornelis harvesting sugar beets, recently cultivated by order of Napoleon.

When Holland became part of France, my grandfather (3) was no longer a day laborer but a _journalier_ !

N. d'ordre de chaque commune.	NOMS.	PRÉNOMS.	Date de la Naissance.	Célibataires	Veufs.	Mariés.	d'Enfans.	de vieux parens à leur charge.	Profession.
				Indication s'ils sont			Nombre		
175	Poortvliet	Cornelis	16 avr. 1707	.	.	—	.	..	journalier

CONTRIBUTION

DES PORTES ET FENÊTRES DE 1812

Numéros de la Matrice Cadastrale des Propriétés bâties.	NOMS ET PRENOMS des PROPRIETAIRES	NOMBRE DES				Répartition du contingent.
		Portes et Fenêtres des rez-de-chaussée 1.re et 2.e étages.	Fenêtres du troisième étage et au dessus.	Portes et Fenêtres des Maisons n'ayant qu'une Porte et une Fenêtre	portes cochères et charetières.	
152	Poortvliet (Cornelis) N° 175	8				

The things those French thought up!

And my grandfather (3) had to pay a tax on his doors and windows!

Although they expected us to understand French, they couldn't even make the postal stamp for Dirksland correctly! Ha!

On top of all that, a ponteneur, an ordinary customs man, would walk through your street as though he was Napoleon himself.

140

They had eight doors and windows.
No chicken wire. That only arrived in 1893.
Oil lamps didn't appear until 1870.

But that didn't bother them much.
Even the French could be tolerated. What really tormented them, though, was that none of their children could stay alive.

Apothecary's wares, quack medicines, and donkey's milk did nothing to change the situation.

Laying their stockings in the form of a cross when they went to bed didn't help either.

1815 THE BATTLE OF WATERLOO

and Maatje is born, and thank God she stays alive!

However, she only lived to be nineteen years old.

The medical profession didn't amount to much in those days. If infectious diseases were going around, people would sprinkle vinegar in front of the bed. In order to avoid infection himself, the doctor would smoke a pipe of strong tobacco.

People would put a dog in bed with a child who had a "weak chest" so that the dog could take over the ailment.

No. 1816.

Op den 7den Juny, zyn, op Belydenis des Geloofs, tot Ledematen aangenomen:

— 1. Jacoba Gardenier . . . .
— 2. Johanna van de Gevel } E.L.
— 3. Jan Manenberg . . . .
— 4. Pieternella Visser } E.L.
— 5. Cornelis Pootvliet

excerpt from the Dirksland church register showing the membership of Cornelis Pootvliet

1821 Napoleon dies on St. Helena

142

I never realized that there were only two years between the death of Napoleon and the birth of my great-grandfather (1823).

The terribly severe winter of 1844!
The rain barrel had frozen solid.
The windows had to be thawed with a firepot.

143

After that there was the potato blight, which plunged Goeree - Overflakkee into poverty

Still much poverty.

On September 30, 1851, Elizabeth Groen died at the age of sixty-three, and yet again Cornelis treads the familiar path to the cemetery.

No. 47 Akte van Overlijden van *Elizabeth Groen*

In het jaar een duizend acht honderd een en vijftig, den *veertigsten* der maand *September* zijn voor ons ondergeteekende *Pieter Taaijer Burgemeester* Ambtenaar van den burgerlijken-stand der gemeente D I R K S L A N D, Provincie Zuidholland verschenen: *Johannes Rooizand* oud *Negenenveertig* jaren, van beroep *timmerman, bekende* van den overledenen en *Jacobus van den Hoek* oud *achtenveertig* jaren, van beroep *Schoenmaker, bekende* van den overledenen, wonende beide in deze gemeente, welke ons hebben verklaard, dat op den *veertigsten* der maand *September* duizend acht honderd een en vijftig, des *morgens* ten *acht* ure, in het huis staande in deze gemeente, numero *Honderd Zevenen negentig* is overleden *Elizabeth Groen* van beroep *zonder* geboren te *Oud Beijerland* wonende te *Dirksland* in den ouderdom van *drieen zestig jaren, echtgenoot van Cornelis Poortvliet avonturier wonende te Dirksland, dochter van Gerrit Groen en van Jannetje Fruimkes beide overleden.*

En hebben wij hiervan deze akte opgemaakt, welke, na voorlezing, is onderteekend door ons *en de declaranten*

On February 1, 1855, the undertaker's messenger announced that Cornelis also passed away.

Death Certificate of
Cornelis Poortvliet →

Cornelis died on January 31, 1855,
he was sixty-seven years old,
and his profession was still
listed as "adventurer."

Nº. 5   Akte van Overlijden van *Cornelis Poortvliet*

In het jaar een duizend acht honderd vijf en vijftig,
den *eersten* der maand *february* zijn voor ons ondergeteekende
Pieter Laayer Burgemeester
Ambtenaar van den burgerlijken-stand der gemeente **D I R K S L A N D**, Provincie Zuidholland verschenen: *Cornelis Soldaat* oud *negen en veertig*
jaren, van beroep *avonturier, gebuur* van de overledene
en *Hendrik van Breda* oud *vyf en dertig* jaren, van
beroep *avonturier, gebuur* van de overledene, wonende beide in deze
gemeente, welke ons hebben verklaard, dat op den *een dertigsten* der maand
January duizend acht honderd vijf en vijftig, des *middags* ten *twee* ure, in
het huis staande in deze gemeente, numero *honderd zeven en negentig*
is overleden *Cornelis Poortvliet* van beroep *avonturier* geboren
te *Dirksland* wonende te *Dirksland*
in den ouderdom van *Zeven en Zestig jaren, weduwenaar*
van Elisabeth Groen, zoon van Zacharias Poort-
vliet en van Geertje Kleut, beiden over-
leden,

En hebben wij hiervan deze akte opgemaakt, welke, na voorlezing, is onderteekend door ons
en de declaranten,

P Laayer   *C. Soldaat*
                  H van Breda

My great-great-grandfather left me one tangible item:
his signature!

145

The father of Cornelis,
my grandfather (4)

Zacharias Poortvliet

christened in Dirksland: 10/19/1738
died in Dirksland: 11/28/1807

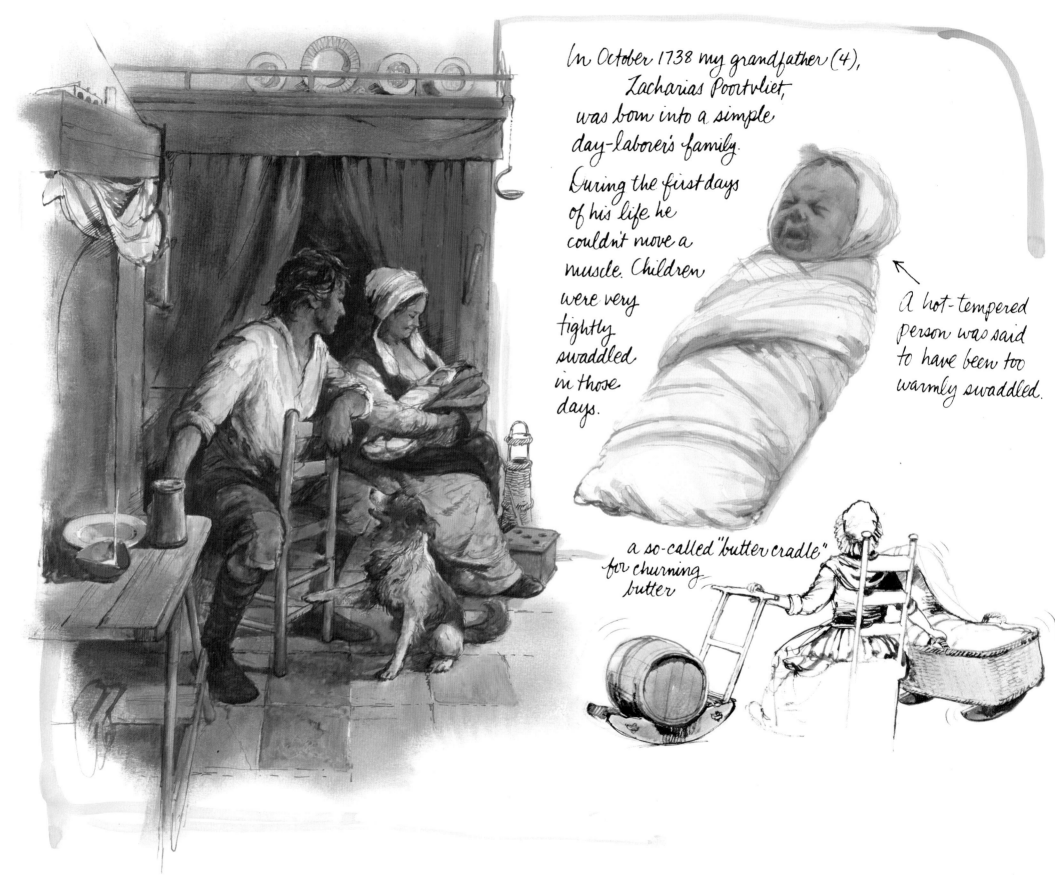

In October 1738 my grandfather (4), Zacharias Poortvliet, was born into a simple day-laborer's family. During the first days of his life he couldn't move a muscle. Children were very tightly swaddled in those days.

A hot-tempered person was said to have been too warmly swaddled.

a so-called "butter cradle" for churning butter

148

The winter of 1740 began mildly enough, but it steadily got colder and colder.

A report of the time says in old Dutch: "Reports come in every day that many people are freezing to death... and some are also found frozen, sitting in the fields."

Hungry packs of wolves in the provinces of Gelderland and Brabant became more and more daring! In 1760 there was a plague of wolves.

149

But Zacharias is inside and doesn't notice the extreme weather conditions (in order to keep him from getting underfoot his mother has put him into the baby pen).

In order to learn to walk, toddlers were put into one of these baskets.

When a toddler began to walk unassisted, he wore this protective helmet.

Zacharias is five years old and the Sinterklaas* songs are still in his head when,

on Sunday, December 8, 1743, a strange star with a tail appeared in the sky— an evil omen! In the cities panic broke out.

* The feast of St. Nicholas (Sinterklaas) on December 5 is a day of celebration in Holland.

150

In 1745 there was widespread cattle plague.

In 1746 the French occupied Sluis and Bergen op Zoom.

In November 1749 Zacharias lost his mother.

He was eleven years old at the time and had to go out and help his father earn a living.

He often worked as apprentice farmhand for the farmer who also employed his father, and you can be sure that those farmers made you work!

Although you have Samson's great strength
And Solomon's wonderful brain,
Working to please a farmer
Is working all in vain.

This verse was on my Uncle Sakries's stable door.

It was quite common to see hardworking children in those days.

A face like this was also a common sight

It wasn't unusual to see women smoking pipes.

Everyone thought it was quite normal for children to treat animals like this and nobody said anything about it.

On this house there was a sign above the door saying:

I live here on the corner
And I could wish no more
Than the blessing of the Lord
And customers at my door.

152

"Scabies teach you how to scratch!"
People weren't very clean in those days.

Often wash your hands and teeth
And sometimes wash your feet;
But let it for all time be said,
You must never wash your head.

FATHER CATS

So with filthy feet and unclean underwear,
our forefathers climbed into bed.

Whole colonies of
mice used to inhabit the
straw mattresses, and
they would keep you
awake with
their noise.
The rug in front
of the bed was
sheep — or
goat
skin.

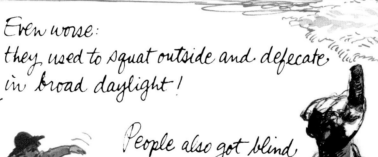

Even worse:
they used to squat outside and defecate,
in broad daylight!

People also got blind
drunk at any hour
of the day —

an enormous
amount of
drinking went on!

⋆ Jacob Cats — famous Dutch
statesman and poet (1577-1660)

But in Amsterdam it was worst of all! There you could go every day to the Dam square and watch criminals being punished. That was entertainment for the people!

‡ AMSTERDAMSCH
HOERDOM,
Behelzende

De liften; daar zig de Heeren en Hoere-Waardinnen van bedienen; benevens derzelver manier van leven, Politique ftreeken, en in 't algemeen alles, 't geen by deze Juffers in gebruik is.

De agtfte Druk verbetert.

Te AMSTERDAM,
Gedrukt voor A. GJOEJET. Boekverkoper aan den Overtoom 1782.

<u>Harlotry in Amsterdam:</u>
a book about prostitutes and what they do.

But what the people of Flakkee thought strangest of all about Amsterdam was that towns people let horses <u>drag</u> a load, when it was obvious that a load on wheels is much easier to move and that a horse could pull much better like this than like this!

1751

When Zacharias was thirteen years old he was allowed to go off with his friends and explore Goedereede on foot!

At that time Westvoorne and Zuidvoorne were joined together by a dam.
(Dirksland had about one thousand inhabitants then.)

OP DE VOLCKERACK

156

Boys of thirteen or thereabouts were welcome to come and look around,

but young lads a-courting had better stay away!!

Fortunately, Zacharias got to know
a girl from his own village
and married when he was thirty-one—
very late for those days.

1769
den 20 Jann: Ondertrouwt
Zacharias Poortvliet J: M.
getrouwt den
19 Febr:
Geertje Kluyt J: D
bij de hier geboren en wonende

notice of marriage of Zacharias and Geerje Kluyt

157

On December 30, 1770, Maatje, their first child, was christened. (The following day was also festive—doughnuts are traditionally eaten on New Year's Day.)

Maatje only reached the age of two and a half.
All their children were to die young.
The only survivor was my grandfather (3) Cornelis, their tenth child.

Thus my grandparents (4) left their house to bury a child _nine_ times.

"There are more calfskins than ox skins going to market," was a saying of the time.

THE LAMENT OF LITTLE WILLEM

ON THE DEATH OF HIS LITTLE SISTER

Alas! my sister is dead,
She was only fourteen months old.
I saw her lie dead in her coffin:
My poor little sister was cold!
I called to her "dear little Mietje!"
"Mietje!" but to no avail.
Alas! her eyes stayed shut;
With bitter tears I now must wail.

from _Children's Poems_ by Hieronymus van Alphen, 1778

February 10, 1781

My grandfather is conscripted into the Dirksland home guard.

De burger wagt van Dirksland

Tot Adelborsten benoemd en aan
gesteld de volgende perzonen.

Leendert Olijman
Cornelis Kruytloff
Anthony de Wit
Dingeman vanden Sluis
Jan Ranke
Jan Looij
Zacharias Poortvliet

According to the army museum my grandfather must have worn this
uniform, but the orders for the Dirksland patrol say that no one
should appear on guard duty wearing clogs or in a state of inebriation.

Niemand Zal met houte klompen aen de voeten
op de wagt moeen koomen off Heren Wildexen

Niemand Zal vermogen dronken ter wagt te koomen

I'm afraid that the Dirksland home guard were not exactly model
soldiers!

1787
April
Den 22sten

Het kind Cornelis
Vader Zacharias Doortvliet
Moeder Geertje Lugt
Getuige Pieternella Doortvliet

Their tenth child, my great-great grandfather, is christened in 1787.

1795, the year of the "velvet revolution"

French occupation.

Requisition of horses on Flakkee

About one hundred and fifty years later the Germans would be doing exactly the same thing.

Fertile DIRKSLAND, ancient town,
Lies in fields of green and brown,
Pleasant and clean with a harbor too—
Which gives both trade and a beautiful view.

In 1798 a lady sat on the Oosthaven dike in Dirksland, drawing a picture, and that would certainly have been noticed by the villagers!

Anna Brouwer was drawing an illustration for the book entitled Descriptions of Towns and Villages.

Datum der Aangeving.	Datum van 't Overlijden.	Naam.	Ouderdom.	Precise Woonplaats.
1807 Novemb 21	21 Nov?	Pieter Zoon van Bastiaan Jongebloed en Cornelia Källe	6 as M.	Dirksland
28	28 Otto	Zacharias poortvliet	70 Jaar	

On November 30, 1807, the funeral of Zacharias takes place.
Zacharias is the son of grandfather (5).

Cornelis Simonsz poortvliet

1709-1772

Cornelis Simonsz Poortvliet was born in 1709.
He was twenty-three years old when this farmhouse, called "Bouwlust," was built near Oude Tonge.
The farmhouse is still there.

The built-in bed in the maid's room is exactly above the cellar entrance so that it slopes. But people didn't → mind that in those days because they used to sleep in a half-sitting position anyway.

Superstitious as they were at the time, they thought it was too risky to sleep lying down flat — that was just asking for death, so they slept like this.

They quivered with fright if they heard an owl hooting on the roof.

You didn't pretend to be any braver than you were: if you saw a black cat crossing in front of you, you quickly laid a cross made of sticks on the road.

You couldn't be too careful with black cats.

After all, think of what just happened in Ouddorp. A cheeky black cat was swiped with a hot frying pan. And wouldn't you know it? The next day someone who had long been suspected of witchcraft was seen walking around with a singed head!

Old women also couldn't always be trusted.

There were too many mysterious incidents involving dead pigs and lame horses!

165

Plenty of people had seen with their own eyes how witches would fly off in the evening in the direction of Sommersdijk where a witches's sabbath was reputed to be held in a nearby meadow.

In my grandfather Cornelis Symonsz's day the witches weigh house in Oudewater was not in use for the amusement of tourists!

A simple household test: if you found a ring of feathers in the pillow of a sick child there was witchcraft involved.

A black hen should then be stuck all over with pins and immersed in boiling water so the witch would be forced to reveal herself.

In the same year that "Bouwlust" was built,
a watermill was constructed in Dirksland.

And, Cornelis Symonsz planned to get married, but
he had no money, as is shown by these documents:

1736
24.ᵗ feb

Dirksland,
the beginning
of the Boezem

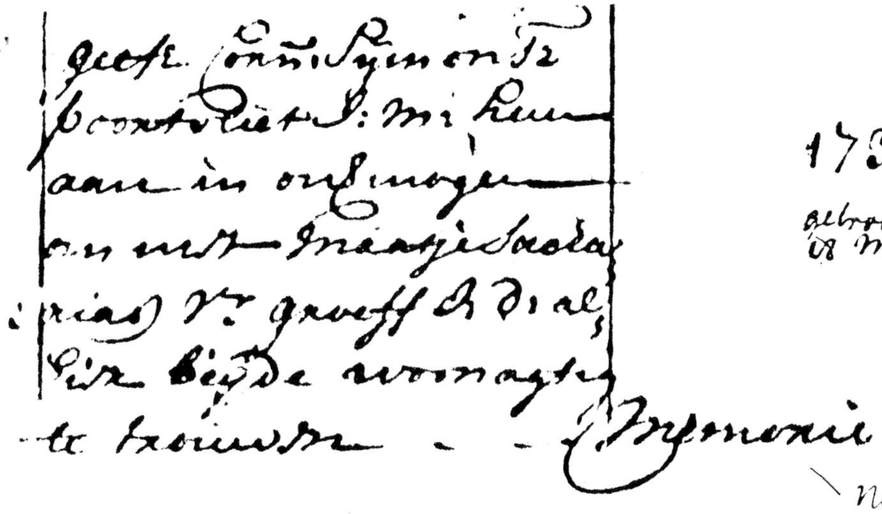

1736

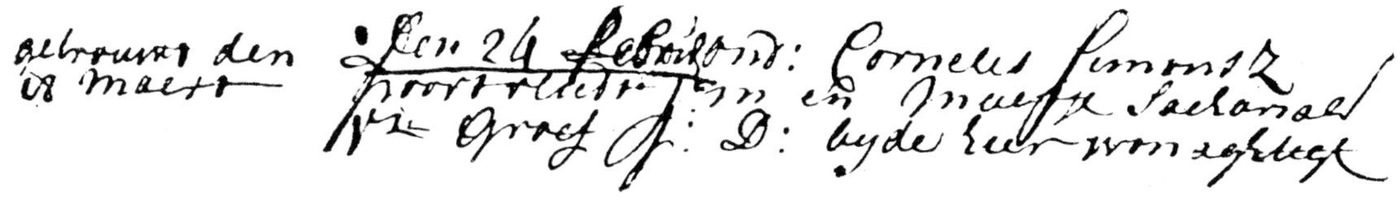

notice states that the marriage was performed
free of charge for "indigents"

167

Most building materials, including the heavy stones for the Dirksland church,
arrived by boat at the Dirksland lock, which now looks like this.

Official statement charging him to care for the welfare, pay for the education and learning of a craft for all five children →

On November 24, 1749, my grandmother (5) Maatje dies. Cornelis is left alone with four children.

Within three months (he must have been on the lookout for someone) he marries one Burgje.

She dies on January 17, 1758.

In March Cornelis Symonsz gets into difficulties.

These are the coins
that my grandfather
so badly needed.

When he marries for the third time
just four weeks later, he is once
again in "a state of indigence" as
stated in the notice of marriage below.

1758

For the Poortvliet children there would be no more lazing around!

From now on they had to go to school under the tuition of schoolmaster Hendrik Schravelaar, one of those who signed this document.

171

Dirksland
school
on the Ring

Rates:
reading lessons: 5 cents per week
reading and writing
lessons: 14 cents
reading, writing, and
arithmetic:
19 cents per week

Hendrik Schravelaar
was schoolmaster, inspector of weights and measures, bread weigher,
gravedigger, and bell ringer from 1729 to 1768 for fl 72 per year.

"Thou who art weary from trudging the road,
Come into the Half Moon and shed thy load!"

This was written above the door of this inn on the dike between Dirksland and Sommersdijk.

My grandfather (5) passed it regularly.
I don't know whether his meager purse would allow him to accept the invitation.

173

Cornelis Simonsz was certainly not the only one with money worries — there was poverty everywhere!

"Under the cloak the rags are hidden" was a saying of the time. Armies of beggars, tramps, and vagabonds (people used to call them "heathens" or "Egyptians" in those days) would drift from village to village.

My grandfather (5) was allowed to earn some extra money — I read this in the church register — by shoveling sand beneath Reverend Bartz's house.

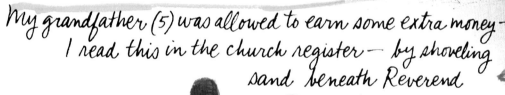

He was about sixty at the time.

On March 23, 1772, the mirror was covered. Cornelis Simonsz Poortvliet was dead.

He himself accompanied two wives and seven children to the cemetery.

174

Psalm C I V

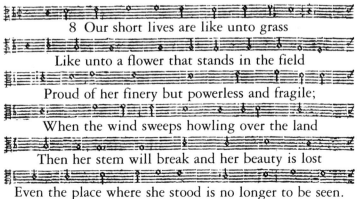

8 Our short lives are like unto grass

Like unto a flower that stands in the field

Proud of her finery but powerless and fragile;

When the wind sweeps howling over the land

Then her stem will break and her beauty is lost

Even the place where she stood is no longer to be seen.

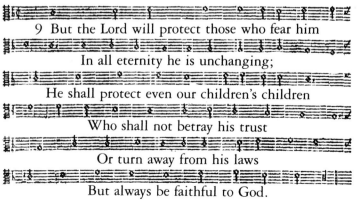

9 But the Lord will protect those who fear him

In all eternity he is unchanging;

He shall protect even our children's children

Who shall not betray his trust

Or turn away from his laws

But always be faithful to God.

Simon Poortvliet

was christened on January 16, 1684, in Colijnsplaat (North Beveland).

When he married Pieternella van der Berge in 1704 everything was just fine.

Four years later the trouble started.

Pieter Belleman   Frans de Neeff   Simon Poortvliet   Adriaentje Munter

Wij Schout ende Schepenen der Prochie ende Heerlijckheijd van Colynsplaet ende noortbevelandt certefiseeren ende verclaren bij desen, dat francois de Neff, synde onsen borger ende Inwoonder, voor ons is gecomen ende gecompareert, te kennen gevende, dat desselfs Huysvrouwe Adriaentie Dircx Munter synde groff swanger tusschen woonsdagh ende donderdagh des nagts, den 3e en 4e april deses Iaers 1709 in stilte is weghgegaen met haer mede nemende den meesten huysraet, een bedde, een copere ketel, twee stucken Linden, veele van desselfs hemden etca mitsgrs: een groote somme gelts: Ende wyders, dat eenen Symon Poortvliet synde aen des comparants huys seer familiaer ende dagelyx converseerende, sigh selven sedert den voorss. tijt heeft geabsenteert, — verlatende syn vrouw en kint, ende sulcx naer alle presumptien auteur van dese desertie, ende amotie syner goederen; en alzoo hy comparant gdresolveert is gdworden desselfs te agtervolgen omuud wadrt mogelyck aen syn weggdvoerd ende ontnomdn goedwdn te gdrakdn, soo heeft hij dese onse certificatie versogt, dwelck wij hdm gdaend hdbben verlddnt, om hdm te dienden dadr hij dese van noodn moqt hdbben, aldus gdaadn den .. april 1709.

In short: Frans de Neeff lodged an official complaint that his pregnant wife had taken French leave and that Simon Pootvliet (his neighbor who always made such friendly visits to his house) had also disappeared.

Frans demanded the return of his property;

he didn't mention Adriaentje.

For some reason that was probably connected with this, my grandfather (6) was taken prisoner in Middelburg.

First he was brought to Colijnsplaat by horse and cart and then by ferry to Veere.

From Veere it was about four miles
to Middelburg—
at least grandfather Simon got
to see some sights.

Maybe he was able to catch a glimpse ↑
of the Court of Zeeland from the
prisoners' cart.

Here Simon was handed over to his jailors at the Gravensteen prison in Middelburg. In that place you had better watch your step—

they didn't have those thumbscrews for nothing!

Pieternella and his parents did what they could for him

March 7, 1710

Statements from character witnesses for Simon, who blame Adriaentje for leading him astray.

Compareerde voor Schepenen van colijnsplaet en koortbeurland ondergenoemt, de ondervolgende persoonen den welke de requisitie ende Versoicke van pieternella pieters Huijs vrouw van Sijmon poortvliet, althans gedetineerde tot Middelburgh mitsgrs: ter instantie ende versoucke van Jas poortvliet des ouder Inde pieternella simons resp. n'vader ende moeder vande, voorn. Sijmon poortvliet. Verclare, voorde opregte Waerhaÿ de welk t'geen hieraenvolgend is opgesteld. namentlÿk

Andries Verburgt out ontrent 54 Jaar verclaart dat oogschijnelijk by verscheijde reijsen heeft gesien dat Adriaentie Dirxse bij wijlen geweest heijst van frans de neve, de gedetineerde Symon poortvliet heeft aenleijding gegeve tot dergelicke familiaere conversatie.

Claes Lievensse out ontrent 40 Jaer, verclaert t'selve als hier voren, en daer mede confirmerende.

Corstiaen Dirxse out 26 jaar verclaard dat langs Jaere met de voors: Symon poortvliet heeft geweest, en noijt gesien en oock bevonden als t'geen eerlijk en betamelijk is,

Pieter Belleman out ontrent 35 jaere verclaert dat inden jaere 1709 frans de neve, en Symon poortvliet met de deponent langs tijt gevrijt hebbende, heeft gesien dat de gem: Adriaentie Dirxse het oock soo wel voor Symon als voor frans bragt soo dat sij t'samen gemeijnelijk spijsigde.

Grietie Zegers out ontrent 27 Jaere verclaard te confirmeren met het voorgestelde van Pieter Belleman en sulx mede oock te hebben gesien

Annetie .... heijst van Hijnd de Roij out 47 Jaer verclaerd dat indie haerweek 1709 de voors: Adriaentie Dirxse des naghts tusschen 11 a 12 uijer aen haer huijs quam kloppe en haer kind en vrage te huijse om een partije goet a drij (dat sij seijde op de straet stond) weg te brengen seggende groten haest hadt mede helpende de paelden inspannen.

Anna Ouÿ des huÿsv. vez corr: goeved out 40 Jaen
verclaerd, dat frans ... aen ... huÿs vraekyde lÿff is
gelomg uÿt naez van sÿ vrouÿd Adraeutie, dat de deponent
bÿ haer zoud komen, voorgevend sulk te werk, dat de
deponent verseÿd rÿsz dat de voorsz adraeutie weed goed

aengeboden, onder althans gedetuceed sÿna pootvliet
verhalen, Snlex de deponentd althoos heeft gewÿgen
frans de rev—, en sÿ adriaentie heff de gedetineerd
alsdaz halende en familjaer daen mede verkeerd.
Wÿders Verclaerd de deponente dat gesien heeft
dat de voorz adriaentie ditby cemig Veugift, legad
genaemt, inde hund haedw seggende haar selcs te
kort to willg does, en het royaal te willg inmdued
de deponent het pampiertie met legaal uÿt haar
hand van en wegsmeet.

Comspareerde mede paternella sÿmons onde paternella
pieters mede, inde brouw vunden gedetineerd
verson ... bdÿse dat de gedetineerd sÿne misgrefz
mogt werda vergeetz, biddend de heeren legters
daer ... en gemad en gees legt etc.

Verclarende alle t'gene voorsz waer en waaragtig te
wÿsz, en des noots t'selv met Eede te
sullen bevestigz, Actum olÿns placet dez 7.de maet
1710 present d'heer daniel rademaker en Jacob
oost ... Schepenen.

Andries Verburgt, aged about fifty-four years, declared that on several occasions he saw that Adriaentje Birxse Munter, the former housewife of Frans de Neeff, did provoke the prisoner Simon Poortvliet, and she provided the opportunity for flirtatious conversation and unseemly behavior.

Claes Lievensse, aged about forty years, declared the same, and he confirmed the above statement.

Corstiaen Veel, aged twenty-six years, declared that he had known the above-named Simon Poortvliet for many long years and that he had never found otherwise than that he is honest and proper in his dealings.

Pieter Belleman, aged about thirty-five years, declared that in the year 1708 Frans de Neeff and Simon Poortvliet worked for a long time together with the witness and that the previously named Adriaentje Birxse brought food for Simon as well as Frans.

Grietie Zegers, aged about fifty-seven years, confirmed the statement of the above-named Pieter Belleman and declared that she also saw it herself.

Jannetie de Roy, housewife of Hijndrik de Roy, aged forty-seven years, declared that in Easter week, 1709, the above-named Adriaentje Birxse came knocking at her door in the night between 11:00 and 12:00, requesting to hire a cart to transport a parcel (which she said was standing on the street). She said she was in great haste and would help to span the horses.

the goings on in the night as described by Jannetje de Roy

The story told by Anna Munters was also dramatic.

Adriaentje was just about to commit suicide by swallowing rat poison when Anna snatched it and threw it away.

Thus various witnesses made statements testifying to the good character of Simon Poortvliet.

Anna Munters, housewife of Cornelis Goeree, aged forty years, declared that Frans de Neeff came to her house on several occasions to fetch her to minister to his wife, Adriaentje, who pretended to be ill, and the afore-named Adriaentje then on several occasions offered the witness money if she would fetch the prisoner Simon Poortvliet, but that the witness always refused to do so. However, Frans de Neeff and Adriaentje often invited the prisoner into their house themselves and they communed with him in a familiar way. Further the witness declared that the afore-named Adriaentje Birxse on one occasion had poison called "regael" in her hand and said that she would kill herself by swallowing the regael. The witness snatched the regael out of her hand and threw it away.

Jan Poortvliet
den Ouden

Pieternella
Simons

Pieternella Pieters

Andries
verhuygt

Cornelisen
Veel

Claes hieuwisse

And they ask the judges
to forgive Simon's mistakes,
to show mercy to him
and not pass judgment.

Grietie Leyers

Pieter Belleman

Jannetie de Roy

Anna Muntelis

It is not known when Simon was set free
and allowed to leave Walcheren.

Herkingen

Was he in trouble? Nevertheless, Simon packed his bags and left Zeeland. And that is how the Pootvliets ended up in Flakkee.

In 1714 he appeared in Dirksland where, as widower of Pieternella, he married Adriana.
They were very poor, and in the →
old village records he was referred to as an "indigent."

11ᵉ decemb. Bill. Prodeo gegeven om Jaymen poort vliets kint alhier te begraven. —Memorie

Den 21 Septbᵉ 1714

getrouwt den xbᵉ 1714

Simon poortvlietb wedr van pieternella van den berg met Adriana Fanins J.d. boide wonende in dit ꝗ

Wedᵉ vanvad: Vaniis

R⁸ 29ᵈ Dito geeft aan Simon poort, Vliet om in den huywelijks staat te traeds met Lijsabet vande Lang, Straat beyde Woonende alhier en Schaat te gegons onder fafy sis van onpmogesdis — Prodo

Den 26ᵉ April 1726, geeft aan Simon poort Vliet om 't lijk Van sijn kint te begraven en Schaat te gegoren onder Clagsis van onpmogendis — Prodo.

Simon died on October 31, 1730, but his rural drama is neatly preserved in the old books.

189

Jan Jansz's signature

190

He can just imagine himself
dressed like that....

and such adorable breeches!

"Look at those silly French monkeys,"
he might have said.

Did Jan Jansz Poortvliet
← look like this? Who can say? At any rate, while he
didn't look as ridiculous as his contemporary Louis XIV,
neither did he look as smart as the gentry.

Little or nothing is known about the clothes worn by
our peasant forefathers.
The working people recycled every last piece of fabric —
none of it survived to appear in a museum.

My grandfather (7) Jan Jansz was probably
also a land worker — a farmhand on a farm like this. I cannot deny that my grandfather is looking rather unfriendly.
His expression asks: "What are you after?"
But don't forget that in those days there was
a lot of riff-raff wandering around!

Were they honest folk coming into the yard
or were they shifty-eyed rascals?
You couldn't always tell at
first glance.

There were
times when you
needed the services
of the Jewish merchant
who sold spectacles
or the rat-catcher.

In addition to the wares you bought you got the most wonderful stories told in vivid detail: Michiel de Ruyter's celebrated voyage to Chatham; the death of Rembrandt; how the de Witt brothers got killed!

And in exchange for providing a bite to eat you got some racy news from out of the neighborhood.

194

In the morning people ate bread with breakfast fish (fried smelt) and an egg fried in oil; to drink they had warm or cold beer or sometimes buttermilk.

Maatje takes the plates out of the plate rack.

Whatever was left over in the barrel from the Sunday's salted meat was heated up for the midday meal, together with fried onions, bacon, brown beans, vegetables, "prollepot" with groats, and of course bread because people used to eat with a knife and a hunk of bread.

A fork was hardly ever used, and a spoon was for ladling out the portions.

195

The spoon was only picked up
briefly to scrape up the
last juices on the plate and
then was passed on to the next person.

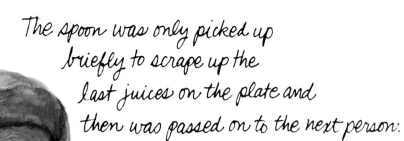

After the meal the Bible was read, and
a psalm would be sung.

Only father and mother sat down at the table —
the children had to stand up.

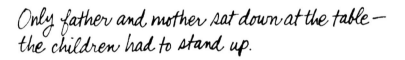

Besides the Holy Scripture, people liked
to read from the works of Father Cats.

There was no bookstore in Colijnsplaat—books were bought at the door from the book peddler.

He also sold waxed slates and ABC planks for schoolchildren.

They didn't learn a great deal at school: first the alphabet, then the Ten Commandments, morning and evening prayers, prayers before eating, the chief articles of the Christian faith, and also some arithmetic.

Perhaps altogether it was more than children learn at most schools these days.

ABC plank

Aa bcdefgh ij
klmnopgrz ſs
tuvwxyz. &c.

A z b n c r d w e b f u g
t h ſ ſ j g k r l z m g
n p o ſ ſ ſ ſ ſ ſt. & &c.

ABCDEFGHIKLMN
OPQRSCUVWXYZ.

197

"They shall sing
Psalms with
clear voices"

And they also sang the hymns composed by Valerius, who was the mayor of Veere:
"Oh Lord, who opens the pavilions of Heaven,"
"Happy is the land," etc.

And of course
when they are allowed
to put their shoes in front →
of the hearth they sang:

"Sinterklaas, good holy man
Put your best tabard on."*

* On the feast of Saint Nicholas,
patron saint of children,
Dutch children place their shoes
by the fire so that the saint can
fill the shoe with gifts while
they sleep.

And there was also a lot of singing at the wedding (1670)
of Jan Jansz and Pieternella.
Here you see my grandfather (7) enjoying his bridegroom's pipe.

199

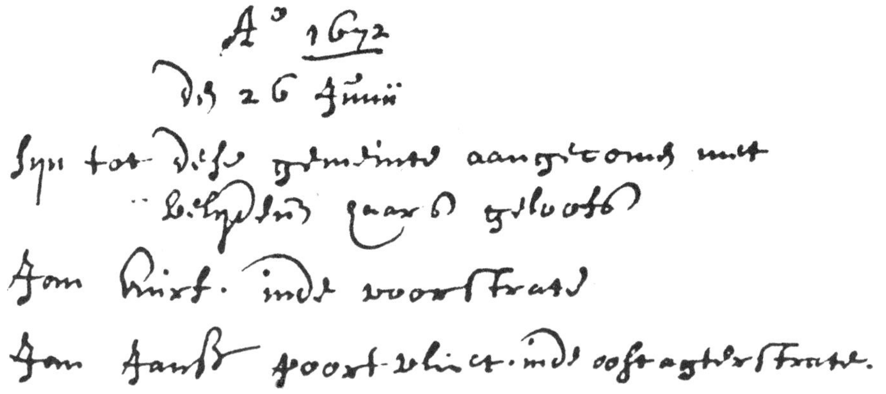

A⁰ 1672
d:, 26 Junii

[handwritten Dutch text]

A 1672

the 26th June

The following persons have professed their faith and
become official members of the congregation.
Jan Linxt from the Voorstraat
Jan Jansz Poortvliet from the Oostagterstraat

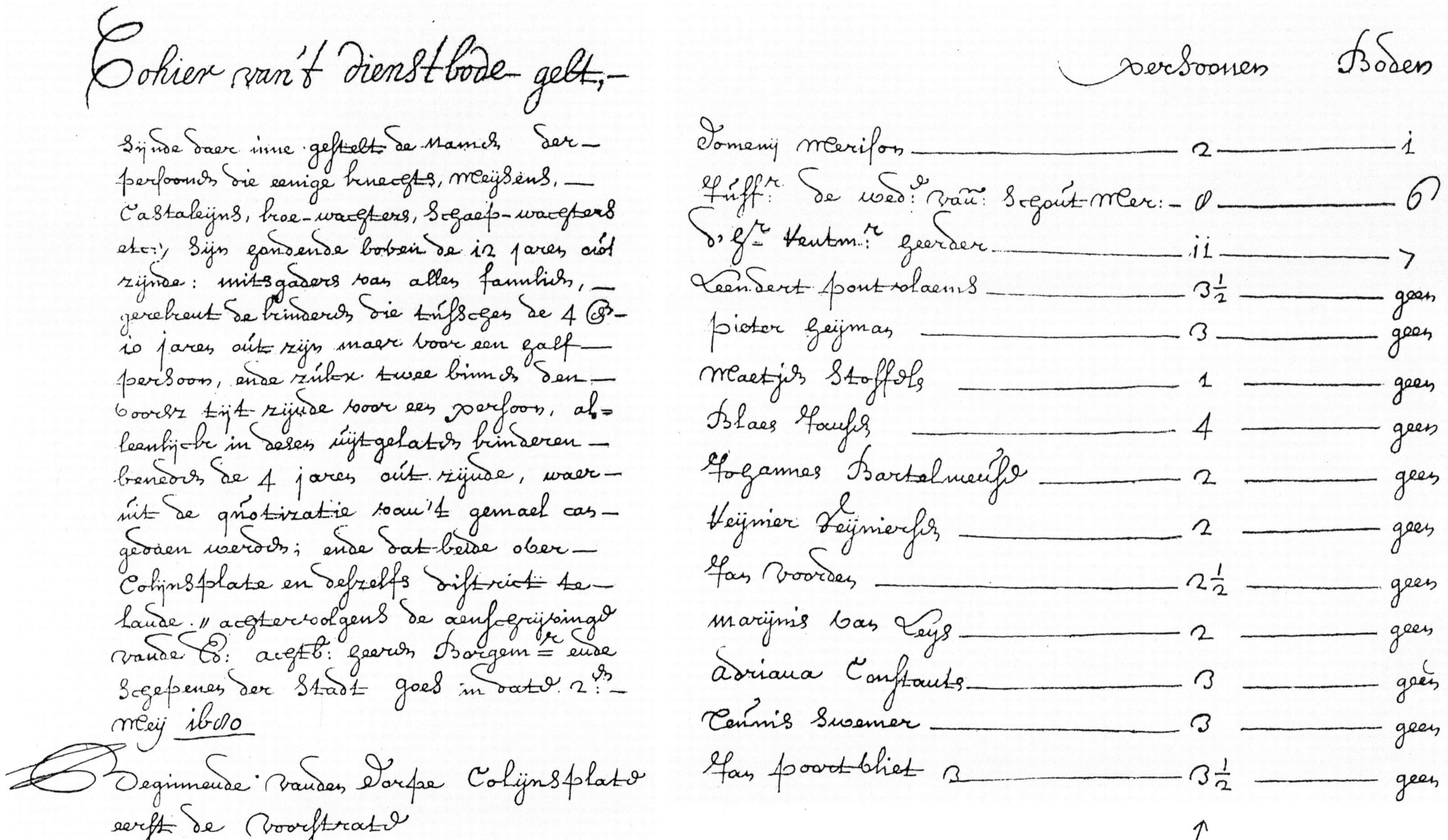

Cohier van 't dienstbode gelt,—

[handwritten Dutch paragraph]

Zijnde daer inne gestelt de namen der
persoonen die eenige knechts, meijssens,
Castaleijns, hoe-wachters, schaep-wachters
etc:, zijn houdende boven de 12 jaren out
zijnde: mitsgaders van alle familien,
gerekent de kinderen die tusschen de 4 @
10 jaren out zijn maer voor een half
persoon, ende zulcx twee binnen den
voorsz tijt zijnde voor een persoon, al-
leenlijcke in desen uijtgelaten kinderen
beneden de 4 jaren out zijnde, waer-
uit de quotizatie van 't gemael ca.
gedaen werden; ende dat bede over
Colijnsplate en deszelfs district te
lande. // achtervolgens de aenschrijving
vande E: achtb: heeren Borgem = ende
Schepenen der Stadt goes in dat. 2:
meij 1680

Beginnende vanden Dorpe Colijnsplate
eerst de Voorstraet

	Persoonen	Boden
Domenij Meerison	2	i
Juffr: de wed: van Schout-Mr:	0	6
D Hr Rentmr: Geerder	ii	7
Leendert Pont Slaems	3½	geen
Pieter Heijmas	3	geen
Maetjes Stoffels	1	geen
Blaes Haufs	4	geen
Johannes Bartelmeusz	2	geen
Heijnier Heijniersz	2	geen
Jan Voorden	2½	geen
Marijns vas Leijs	2	geen
Adriana Constants	3	geen
Tennis Susener	3	geen
Jan Poortvliet 3	3½	geen

father, mother, and three children

200

Their seventh child was my grandfather (6)
Simon (1684).
The following year Johann Sebastian
Bach and Georg Friedrich Händel
were born.

The cane chair was called
a "bakermat," a special
chair in which to nurse
the baby. That green
contraption is a
diaper drier.

In 1688 Jan paid back the money that he borrowed from the
poor relief fund together with the interest:

drig Noben? 1688

outfang? vay say Soortvliet oors set
gus? ден in siju noot was geleent
ded 5 ndij 1686 sijnde set rostant
met dr intrest sama £1:11:4

10 November 1688

Received from Jan Poortvliet the sum lent to him in his
time of need on 5th May 1686 plus the interest over that
sum which amounts to £1.11.4.

(One pound, eleven shillings, four groats)

1695

der 13 Novemb?
aray Mande middags £2:8:9:

Oufongen van San poorvest
de toter pord dit the asm so
gods Brief von typo soys? gelde
test coord in der £2:8:0
suroe est von diez.

In 1695 grandfather (7) became a home owner.
He received a so-called pay-out letter (mortgage) on his
house from the church poor relief fund.

1695
13 November

Received from Jan Poortvliet the two pounds paid by the
poor relief for the letter on his house and the interest.

Mow and harvest, fill the barn
With the products of the farm,
Shear the sheep and squeeze the udders
Seven children and a wife
This is a man's daily life.

An old rhyme describing the life of the
ordinary man. Jan Jansz Poortvliet's life would
not have been much different from this.

my grandfather (8)

Jan Cornelis̆ poȯtⱥⱡie̊t

would have been born around
the same time as Rembrandt
van Rijn — 1606.

It seems that
Jan Cornelisz was a
respectable fellow.

(You didn't get written
about in church records
unless you had
strayed from the path
of righteousness.)

This is the village
where he lived:

Colijnsplaat.

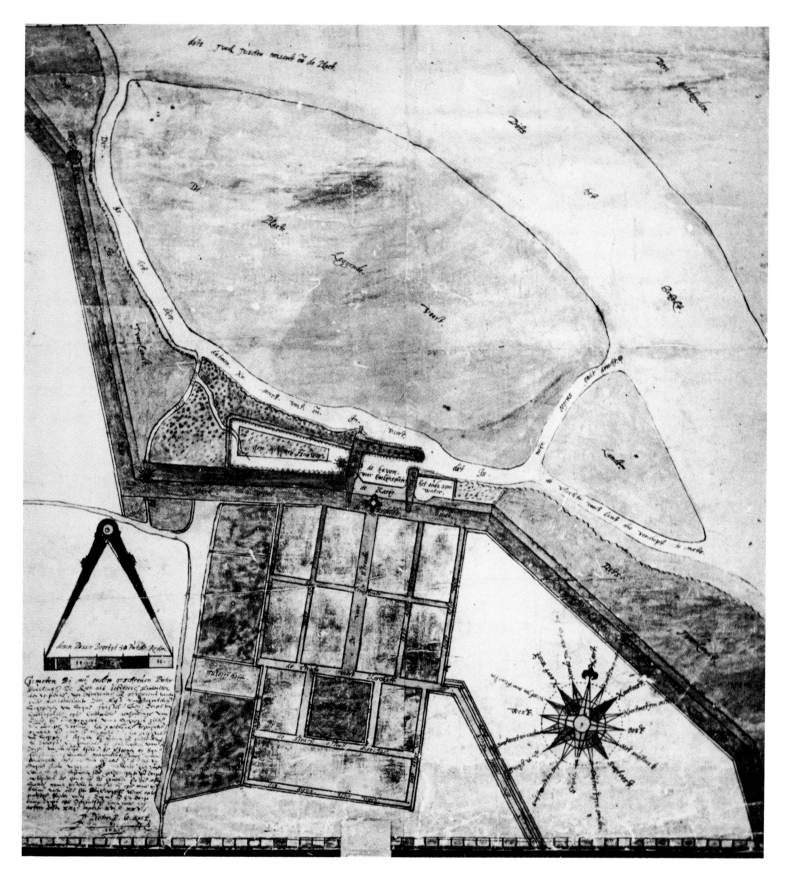

205

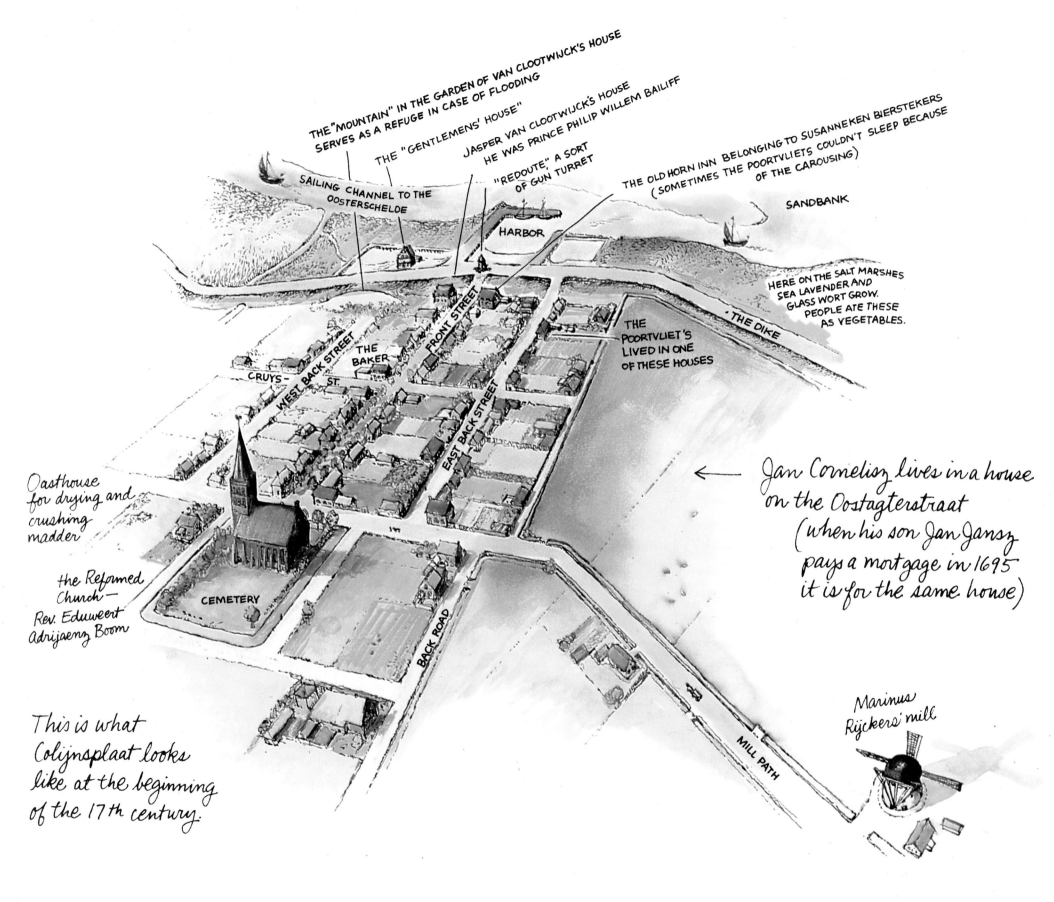

THE "MOUNTAIN" IN THE GARDEN OF VAN CLOOTWIJCK'S HOUSE
SERVES AS A REFUGE IN CASE OF FLOODING

THE "GENTLEMENS' HOUSE"

JASPER VAN CLOOTWIJCK'S HOUSE
HE WAS PRINCE PHILIP WILLEM BAILIFF

"REDOUTE," A SORT
OF GUN TURRET

THE OLD HORN INN BELONGING TO SUSANNEKEN BIERSTEKERS
(SOMETIMES THE POORTVLIETS COULDN'T SLEEP BECAUSE
OF THE CAROUSING)

SAILING CHANNEL TO THE
OOSTERSCHELDE

HARBOR

SANDBANK

HERE ON THE SALT MARSHES
SEA LAVENDER AND
GLASS WORT GROW.
PEOPLE ATE THESE
AS VEGETABLES.

THE DIKE

THE
POORTVLIET'S
LIVED IN ONE
OF THESE HOUSES

FRONT STREET

THE
BAKER

CRUYS-
ST.

WEST BACK STREET

EAST BACK STREET

Oasthouse
for drying and
crushing
madder

the Reformed
Church—
Rev. Eduweert
Adrijaenz Boom

CEMETERY

BACK ROAD

Jan Cornelisz lives in a house
on the Oostagterstraat
(when his son Jan Jansz
pays a mortgage in 1695
it is for the same house)

MILL PATH

Marinus
Rijckers' mill

This is what
Colijnsplaat looks
like at the beginning
of the 17th century.

206

This was the building style of that time (c. 1600).

People wanted an improvement on the wooden houses, which were too flammable. When it came to building pioneers' settlements such as Colijnsplaat, they were thorough.

This is an extract from building regulations of the time:

"a reasonably solid house with at least a stone wall at the front and stone fireplaces and chimneys."

207

Only a few large houses were built:
for example, Bailiff van Clootwijck's
house and Rev. Boom's house.

Most of the houses
looked like this. ——→

Here Rev. Boom is standing in his back
garden thinking up a severe sermon.

The hanging food safe was out of the reach of vermin.

The handsome furniture in the baliff's house...

and here are my forefathers' household possessions.

209

cane chair

wedge chair

armchair

corner chair

triangular chair

barrel chair

baby chair

sermon chair

(for bringing to church)

folding table

footstool

three-legged stool

barrel table

support

(for the washtub, etc.)

cupboard

turf box

candle box

food chest

rocker for cradle

field bed

This is the sort of furniture they had then

The fireplace was very important!

cooking + heat + light

In the mornings there was always the anxious question: is there still life under the ashes? Otherwise you had to go to the neighbours to fetch some glowing coals.

On the floor of the hearth was the grate or two firedogs with which you could make a spit (a fatty joint could baste itself)

The fuel was turf, wood, and cowdung

ashtray

After use, glowing charcoal was put into the extinguisher — the charcoal could be used later in a warming pan.

In the chimney hangs a hook → from which you could hang a cooking pot or the panholder for warming up a dish.

red-hot pot hanger

The barns and sheds belonging to the Voorstraat house ↓

My grandfather (8) Jan Cornelisz standing in front of his house. In the winter the street was such a muddy mess that it was decided that two "street crossings" would be built so that people could cross the street and stay dry.

It was a regulation that people had to scrub the pavement in front of their houses on Saturday.

Inside everything was quite pleasant, but outside it was a mess in the Oostagterstraat — there was "a four-foot-wide brick path" along the front of the houses, but the main street was mud.

The back garden was used for growing vegetables for the family's own consumption

and it also housed the outhouse and the pigsty.

The surgeon and bloodletter Adriaen Bluickvliet would then take inside the two bowls of blood that he kept outside his house on weekdays for advertisement.

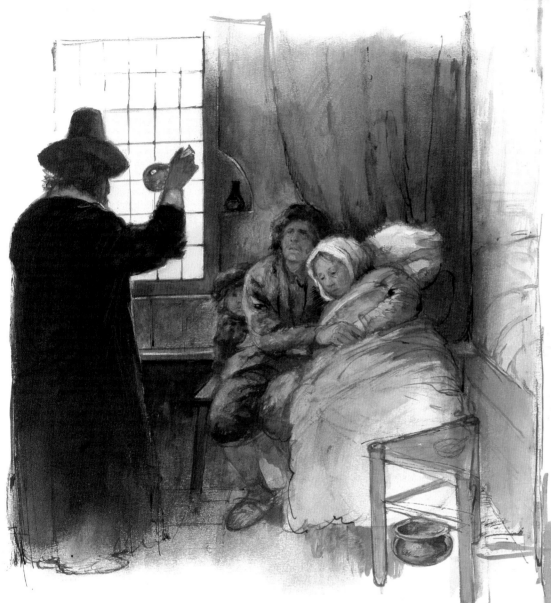

These were all the weapons he had when in 1625 he had to battle the Hot Sickness.

But one after the other the people died from the plague.

In the mornings the bodies were simply dragged outside next to the front door.

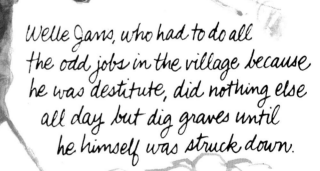

Welle Jans, who had to do all the odd jobs in the village because he was destitute, did nothing else all day but dig graves until he himself was struck down.

Bloodletting and still more bloodletting... apart from that, surgeon Bluickvliet did what he could, and that wasn't much: feeling the pulse, examining the urine, and looking important.

For Minister Boom the coming of "God's righteous punishment, well-earned by this village of Colijnsplaat and the entire island," was not unexpected.

"Supping and carousing and vile lechery, indecent jesting, fighting, and scandalous festivities on the Day of the LORD!"

He loved a fierce sermon!

Schipper Eelleboo ↓

Although nobody's name was mentioned in the sermon it was quite clear to everyone that the minister was referring to Barbel Thonis and her wanton daughter.

In the middle of the sermon Barbel rushed up to the pulpit and shouted that the Rev. Boom himself

"did seek indecency and commit it on her own person."

This "disgraceful behavior" and the murder that resulted caused tongues to wag for a long time.

↑

Eelleboo, Nellken's husband, murdered one of his shipmates during his watch with a "dagger thrust" because the man, loose-tongued with drink, had said that Eelleboo's wife was promiscuous whenever her husband was at sea.

214

That was entertainment for
the people!
It must have given the
family plenty to gossip
about:

Barbel being
thrown out of the
church by the
elders!

There were also other interesting
happenings at that time: the execution
of Oldenbarneveldt (1619), the end of the twelve-year
truce, and the clever escape of Hugo de Groot in 1621.
But none of this was a patch on the business with Barbel!

The era of Jan Cornelisz Poortvliet was also the
era of d'Artagnan of The Three Musketeers.
But if you had happened to meet them together
you could immediately see who was who
because Jan was one of the poor folk, the day
laborers, peasants, and dike workers, and they
didn't lead such a flamboyant existence.

This is your lesson:
Get up at six
And eat ten tens
It will do you good.
And at six again
Lay down your knife
And sleep ten tens
It will do you good.

Jacob Cats

There were about twenty fishermen.

Most men on Colijnsplaat worked on the land.

There were two bakers.
← Herman Geertsz

Theunken Baerentsz Oecker, butcher and roof mender

Dick Lodewijksz, the cartwright

Jan Hubrechtsz Houte, the smith

three carpenters

217

He has won the Silver fleeeeeeeeet!

(*line from a patriotic Dutch song*)

In the year 1628 the admirers of Piet Hein had cause for great celebrations!

The following year Jan Cornelisz Pootvliet married Neelken — and that was another occasion for a good old knees-up.

Anno 1637.
Den 4. Ianuarij

Sijn aengecomen met belijdenisse der geloofs
tot dese Gemeijnte.

Gillis Goderts, J.M. comt van Nort Altwilderschuestt.

Jan Vermaeds, J.M. van loingen in Vlaenderen; ts huis
liggende bij Jacob Gillisz van Orisant.

Theunis Barents, wonende achter de kerck in het
huit van hendrick de Vriese.

Overleden den 7. Decemb. 1650.   Jan Cornelisz poortvliedt, wonende in de oostagherstraet.

Adriaen, their first baby,
was christened on October 13, 1630.

Jan Cornelisz poortvliedt. Neeltkz Adriaenn.		Adriaen	Cornelis van Haghe. Zachariesz Jong malitz. Sebastiaenn. Jacomijntz Cornelis.

Baptismal witness

The baptismal certificate for my grandfather (7).
He is christened on June 19, 1650.
    Six months later, on December 7, 1650,
Jan Cornelisz died.

Jan Corinelisz Poortvliedt Cornelia Adriaenn		Jans	Maidtsn Cornelisz Rochusz Gelderts.

my grandfather (9)

Cornelis
Adriaensz
poortvliet

I found him at the beginning of
the Golden Age in the company of
an army of dirty-looking fellows—
the dike-builders of Colijnsplaat.

They were rough customers who had come from all over the place like flies to a honeypot for the chance of a job. They earned twelve five-cent pieces a day. It wasn't pleasant work but:

He who doesn't toil shall not eat

said Father Cats, who had a law practice in Middelburg, not far away.

It was safer to stay away from the dike unless you had business there! When the dike reeve made his fortnightly inspection, the workers had to stand at a distance of at least two roods from him.

The dike workers were also not allowed to bring daggers or poniards to work.

From time to time the sheds where the workers lived were searched for weapons.

In the sheds a lot of drinking went on, and fights would break out on the slightest pretext.

Anno 1610

Anno 1610

The following persons have joined this community on this day the 10th April, namely Cornelis Adriaensz Poortvliet, Matheus Jaspersz and the wench Pieterse Eliasz.

Hugo de Groot

Han Pietersz Sweelinck

Peter Paul Rubens

Spinola

Joost van den Vondel

Jacob Cats

Johan van Oldenbarneveld

These are all contemporaries of my grandfather (9) Cornelis. They might have been with him on April 10 if they had wanted to.

When the polder and the dike were completed some of the dike workers stayed on in Colijnsplaat.

the white-backed cow

Zealand goat

They managed to get permanent jobs on one of the newly built farmsteads.

That is probably what happened to Cornelis, too.

6/28/1620

After work he often visited a tavern. There were three or four of them.

An excerpt from the church records shows that Cornelis was excluded from the service because of drunkenness.

My grandfather Cornelis Adriaensz was a thirsty man.

9/6/1620

[handwritten text in old Dutch]

Several of the Brethren were annoyed by the behavior of Cornelis Adriaensz and have requested that he improve his behavior.

But he wasn't the only one. Everyone, big and small, drank a lot of beer in those days — drinking water was scarce and often contaminated.

2/7/1621

[handwritten text in old Dutch]

Because Cornelis Adriaensz continues in his drunkenness, in spite of his previous promises, he has been forbidden entry to the service until he behaves in a Christian fashion.

And before you knew it, you had had one too many.

That Vincent Pietersz is either an annoying busybody or one of the church notables... or both.

6/6/1621

[handwritten text in old Dutch]

Because Vincent Pietersz met Cornelis Adriaensz in a state of drunkenness on the Weelsteenshof, it was decided that both he and his housewife shall be refused entry to the church service.

The Rev. Rotarius's handwriting.
He was the successor to the Rev. Boom. →

The quarrel with Frans Wecksteen
ended up in a fight.

—

When Cornelisz Adriaensz
remarried Magdelena
van Gelder, the wedding
party was also not without
incident.

*Consistorie gehouden den
4. November, A°. 1635.*

[handwritten Dutch text]

The Brethren have agreed to summon Cornelis Poortvliet in
front of the church council in order to punish him for his unseemly
conduct toward Frans Wecksteen in a certain tavern. This incident
renewed the same grievance that had previously been apparently resolved
when they had been allowed to attend the church together.

11/4/1635

*Consistorie gehouden
den 7. feb. A°. 1638.*

[handwritten Dutch text]

The Brethren have agreed that Jan van Asperen should be reprimanded
for his unseemly conduct at Cornelis Adriaensz Poortvliet's
wedding party.

7/2/1638

Jan
van
Asperen

at Poortvliet's wedding reception

229

[handwritten facsimile:]
Consistorie gehouden den
6. April, A⁰. 1641.

Cornelis Adriaensz van poortvliedt, ende Magdalena Willems sijn
huisvrouwe is mede van de broeders belast voor desen tijt uijt te
blijven van het Avondtmael des heeren, ende dat van wegen
eenige onlangs gegevene ergernisse.

Cornelis Adriaensz Poortvliet and Magdalena Willems,
his housewife, are temporarily barred by the Brethren
from attending the church service and this because of the
offense and annoyance recently caused by them.

4/6/1641

In 1639 Maarten Harpertsz.
Tromp destroys the Spanish Armada!
Splendid!
All is not well in Magdelena
and Cornelis's marriage —
just peruse the church records!

[handwritten facsimile:]
Consistorium gehouden
den 24. Sept. A⁰. 1645.

Naerdemael men verstaen heeft dat Cornelis Adriaensz van portvliet
ende Magdalena van Gelder sijn huisvrouwe, niet op behoorlicke wijse
'tsamen huis en houden, maer verscheiden eten ende drincken, ende van
malcanderen slapen, soo is goodgeolt dadruad te vernemen ende
haer boide daer over aen te spreken.

Since it has been understood that Cornelis Adriaensz
Poortvliet and Magdalena van Gelder, his housewife, are not
living together in a proper fashion, but eat and drink
separately and sleep apart from each other, the Brethren
have decided to speak to both of them on this subject.

9/24/1645

Consistorium gehouden
den 25. Martij, A°. 1646.

[Dutch handwritten text]

The fashion in which Cornelis Adriaensz Poortvliet and his housewife are living together and also the household of Maycken Jacobs and her husband Lodewyck Hubrechtsz Schipper have shown no improvement and therefore it has been decided to exclude both couples from the church for the time being.

3/25/1646

1646

was also the year in which Punch was born — he and Judy, his wife, were to form a notorious couple.

Consistorium gehouden
den 3. feb. A°. 1647.

[Dutch handwritten text]

The Brethren have agreed to speak to Cornelis Adriaensz Poortvliet about his drinking and his offensive behavior on the day of the previous service.

2/3/1647

← Perhaps Cornelis had been misbehaving during the cold fair in January (there was also a warm fair in the summer).

barred once again

After the wholesale revelry during the fair the Brethren really should have reprimanded everyone for their unseemly behavior!

boozing, guzzling, and carousing

The wenches slept with a wet cloth around their necks on the night before the fair so that they could take part in the festivities with necks unmarred by fleabites.

There was no fair without a market—
you could buy a horse or a new Sunday hat; you could even
have your rotten tooth extracted,

or have your head-lice problems examined
by an expert.

The people looked at
everything with eyes
wide as saucers!

"The things folks
do to earn money!"

233

People had saved their money for six months for this fair, and they wanted to enjoy everything there was to enjoy — the acrobats, the dancing bear, the fortune teller, the dancing, and the carousing, right up to and including the fights with which the fun always ended.

(For slashing faces there were knives with sharp, rounded tips.)

6. Iulij, A° 1647.

[Dutch manuscript text]

It has once again come to the Brethren's notice that Cornelis Adriaensz Poortvliet and his housewife are living with one another in an unseemly fashion, sleeping and eating separately, so that it has been decided to bar them from the service for the time being in order to avoid offense.

7/6/1647

And the fights between Cornelis and Magdalena continued.

Den 29. Martij, A° 1648.

[Dutch manuscript text]

The Brethren on their rounds in the village have also been requested to inquire into the manner in which Cornelis Poortvliet is keeping house with his wife.

3/29/1648

Consistorium gehouden
Den 3. April A° 1649.

[Dutch manuscript text]

They have also reported that they have punished Cornelis Adriaensz Poortvliet and his housewife because of their unchristian household and once again both of them have been excluded from attending the service.

4/3/1649

Thus my grandfather was often found in the tavern. There he could talk about the good old days or hear interesting tidbits of news from foreign Signeurs who dropped into the Old Horn.

And then there were the stories told by the seafaring men just back from a voyage — tales of how they sailed with their Dutch East India Company ship to Africa to pick up a cargo of heathens! Scurvy, keel-hauling, pirates... those were good stories!

And Cornelis had another drink on tick (credit) even though it meant yet another notch on the stick with which the publican kept tally of his bill.

236

The Brethren did not confine themselves to speaking severely to Cornelis —

he was also given money by the church
every fortnight, from
August 1647 to August 1649!

These were the last two years of his life.

On August 20, 1649, my grandfather (9)
Cornelis Adriaensz Pootvliet is buried.

The bell tolled twice every thirty minutes,
and that cost three shillings.

The rental of the large black funeral cloth
amounted to three shillings and four groats.

I have an idea that my grandpa (9)
was a nice grandpa.

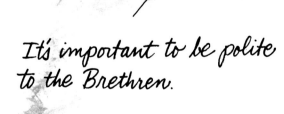

It's important to be polite
to the Brethren.

Adriaen
poortbliedt

238

My grandfather (10), who was born in about 1560, was called Adriaen.

That is all I know about him — there the past comes to an end.
All documents dating from before 1600 were burned during a bombardment in Middelburg in 1940.

Perhaps Adriaen lived in the village of Poortvliet on the island of Tholen
and was driven away from there by the All Saints Flood of November 1570
that caused such terrible destruction.
Who knows?
My grandfather Adriaen could have told me all about the resistance against the Spanish, about
Willem van Oranje (the first William of Orange), the relief of Leiden...
all the people and events in his time.

When this book was finished (there were no more pages) I drove to Zeeland.
In the village of Poortvliet I studied the Old Reformed Church from the outside and from the inside.
I even secretly played some notes on the organ.

In Colijnsplaat I walked down the Oostagterstraat (which is now called Irenestraat)
as far as the church, just as Cornelis Adriaensz and his family must so often have done.
It was all there; the Voorstraat with the tavern on the corner (The Old Horn is now called
The Partridge) and the Kruisstraat. And on the dike, where Cornelis Adriaensz Poortvliet
struggled with his wheelbarrow, I stood and smoked a pipe and looked out over the
wide water just as my grandfather surely did.

Editor: Joan E. Fisher
Calligraphy: Diane Lynch

Library of Congress Cataloging-in-Publication Data

Poortvliet, Rien.
   In my grandfather's house.

   Translation of: Langs het tuinpad van mijn vaderen.
   1. Poortvliet, Rien. 2. Illustration of books—
20th century—Netherlands. 3. Illustrators—Netherlands
—Biography. 4. Poortvliet family. I. Title.
NC983.5.P66A2 1988   759.9492 [B]   88–6266
ISBN 0–8109–1126–4

Copyright ©1987 Uitgeversmaatschappij J. H. Kok BV—Kampen,
the Netherlands

Published in 1988 by Harry N. Abrams, Incorporated, New York
All rights reserved. No part of the contents of this book may be
reproduced without the written permission of the publisher

A Times Mirror Company

Printed and bound in Spain DLB-27186-88